Praise for THE MULTIPLY METHOD

"Sarah is a leader who multiplies leaders—and that's the kind of leader the world needs more of. *The Multiply Method* isn't just another business book, it's a road map to building a legacy by developing people. If you want to grow a business by growing others, this is the book you've been waiting for."

— **John C. Maxwell**
#1 *New York Times* Bestselling Author +
America's #1 Business Leader

"I've mentored Sarah from the beginning of her career and I'm so proud of how she has mastered the simple skills of networking and is willing to share here in *The Multiply Method*. We are in a people business, which requires more than scripts and how-tos—it searches for authenticity and compassion that Sarah delivers. Take the guesswork out of your game plan and learn from a true master."

—**Donna Johnson**, Veteran Networker,
Lifetime Achievement Award Earner,
and Bestselling Author of
My Mentor Walks on Water and
My Mentor's Radical Love

"I KNEW SARAH ROBBINS before she was *the* Sarah Robbins. She had a brilliant mind then and even more so now. Her new book is not just a great read—*it is an absolute must-read* for our profession."

—DR. DOUG FIREBAUGH
Network Marketing Consultant and Speaker

"IN AN INDUSTRY where too many teach what they've never actually built, Sarah Robbins stands out. She's built it. She's led it. And she knows how to teach it. *The Multiply Method* is a proven playbook for anyone serious about building a real, sustainable network marketing business."

—ROB SPERRY
Network Marketing Consultant and Keynote Speaker

"SARAH ROBBINS's *The Multiply Method* is an incredible resource for network marketers, offering straightforward and effective systems to help create a thriving, sustainable team. With helpful strategies such as reframing prospecting as a warm invitation and transforming conversations into wonderful opportunities, Robbins inspires readers to overcome objections and confidently welcome new members. This book is an absolute treasure for anyone excited to multiply their impact and nurture leaders who foster lasting success."

—TROY DOOLY, The Beachside CEO

"*The Multiply Method* is a game changer for anyone ready to build a thriving business and team. Sarah masterfully shows how authentic conversations can turn curiosity into real opportunity. This book is packed with actionable insights on leveraging social media and, most importantly, multiplying your impact by developing new leaders. If you want to grow your business and empower others to do the same, *The Multiply Method* is your must-read road map."

—**Emily Ford,** Industry Leader and Branding Expert

"If you're looking to build a business with integrity, impact, and actual duplication, then *The Multiply Method* delivers. I've known Sarah Robbins personally for a while now and she is absolutely the real deal."

—**Blake Mallen**
Host of *Direct Selling News SHIFT* Podcast

"Sarah Robbins is the real deal! She leads with heart, teaches from experience, and consistently shows up with a level of integrity and authenticity that's rare in our profession. I've watched her grow into one of the most-respected voices in network marketing—and for good reason. Her insights don't just inspire—they move people to action. This book is a gift to anyone serious about building something meaningful."

—**Jordan Adler,** Author of *Beach Money* and *Network Marketing Millionaire*

THE MULTIPLY METHOD

SIMPLE SYSTEMS FOR BUILDING A SOLID, SUSTAINABLE NETWORK MARKETING TEAM

SARAH ROBBINS

MISSION DRIVEN PRESS

THE MULTIPLY METHOD: Simple Systems for Building a Solid, Sustainable Network Marketing Team

Copyright © 2025 by Sarah Robbins

All rights reserved. No part of this publication may be reproduced, stored in a retrieval system, or transmitted in any form by any means, electronic, mechanical, photocopy, recording, or otherwise, without the prior permission of the publisher, except as provided by USA copyright law.

No patent liability is assumed with respect to the use of the information contained herein. Although every precaution has been taken in the preparation of this book, the publisher and author assume no responsibility for errors or omissions. Neither is any liability assumed for damages resulting from the use of the information contained herein.

Published by Mission Driven Press, an imprint of Forefront Books, Nashville, Tennessee.

Distributed by Simon & Schuster.

Library of Congress Control Number: 2025907333

Print ISBN: 978-1-63763-450-9
E-book ISBN: 978-1-63763-451-6

Cover Design by George Stevens, G Sharp Design, LLC
Interior Design by Mary Susan Oleson, Blu Design Concepts

Printed in the United States of America

25 26 27 28 29 30 [Lake Book] 10 9 8 7 6 5 4 3 2 1

To the dreamers, the doers,
and the difference-makers—
may you multiply your impact,
your influence, and change lives.
May this book serve as a guide
to help you expand your vision,
elevate others, and create
a ripple effect of success
beyond what you have ever imagined.

XX,
Sarah

CONTENTS

ACKNOWLEDGMENTS 13

INTRODUCTION:
An Overview of the Multiply Method 17

CHAPTER 1: Prospecting (The Art of Inviting):
Who to Invite and How 41

CHAPTER 2: Presenting: Sharing Your Business
Powerfully and Professionally 63

CHAPTER 3: Closing: Conquering the Close
and Common Objections 79

CHAPTER 4: Fast Start: Starting New
Distributors Strong, Every Single Time 97

CHAPTER 5: Events: Launching New
Distributors Strong 115

CHAPTER 6: Customer Acquisition and Retention:
How to Get Customers and Keep Them 141

CHAPTER 7: Social Media That Sells:
My Social Media Selling System 163

CHAPTER 8: Leadership Systems
and Duplication: Let's MULTIPLY! 185

CHAPTER 9: Creating Team Culture:
The Glue That Holds the Team Together 201

CONCLUSION:
You Were Made to Multiply! 217

ACKNOWLEDGMENTS

WRITING *The Multiply Method* has been an incredible journey, and I am so grateful to everyone who has been a part of it. This book is not just my story, but the story of all the amazing people who have supported, encouraged, and challenged me along the way. Network marketing is a community-based model, and there is no success without "us."

First and foremost, I want to thank my family. Your unwavering love, belief in me, and endless support have been the foundation on which everything is built. To my husband, Phil, who has been the hero of our hearts and home—thank you for loving me, leading our family so well, always supporting our dream, and praying for and encouraging our team. To my beautiful sons, Gabriel and Judah—no title or achievement even comes close to being your mom. You are my WHY, and I hope someday you are inspired by the work I was able to do from home, being present while building a life our family could be proud of

ACKNOWLEDGMENTS

and leaving a legacy. I love you so much. (When people ask Gabriel what I do for a living, he says, "My mom helps a lot of people.") To my mom, Kris—you introduced me to this business and it's changed our family's lives. It's been a joy to be on this journey with you.

To my incredible team—you are the heart of everything I do. This book is a reflection of your hard work, dedication, and passion. I am forever grateful for your trust, your perseverance, your partnership, and your belief in the systems we've built together. I celebrate your success, and watching you achieve your goals has been the most rewarding part of this journey.

A huge thank-you to my mentors and role models, who have guided me at every step. Your wisdom, experience, and generosity in sharing your knowledge have shaped who I am as both a leader and a person. To Doug Firebaugh, Donna Johnson, Lori Bush, and the great John C. Maxwell—thank you for being my first mentors in this business. I wouldn't be where I am without your insight and encouragement.

To the Network Marketing Inner Circle coaching clients and the Made to Multiply Mastermind—thank you for being part of this powerful community. Your commitment to growth, your dedication to learning, and your passion for building beautiful businesses for your family are what keep me motivated. This book is a direct result of the work we've done together, and I am proud to be a part of your journey.

ACKNOWLEDGMENTS

Lastly, thank *you*, the reader. Whether you're just starting your journey or already building a successful network marketing business, I hope this book helps you take the next step. I wrote it with the belief that with the right systems, anyone can achieve their dreams through this business model. It is the honor of a lifetime to help you "walk out your WHY."

INTRODUCTION

AN OVERVIEW OF THE MULTIPLY METHOD

WHEN THE NEWS came, it felt like the ground had shifted beneath me.

For nearly two decades, we had built something extraordinary: a sales team that shattered records in the network marketing industry. We weren't just another group of people selling products—we were a movement. A force to be reckoned with. They called us the "darlings of direct sales." Through dedication, hard work, and a system that I created and refined over the years, we had grown a sales team that consistently broke barriers, setting records that many thought were impossible. We were doing over $2 billion in annual sales, and we did it in just five years.

When the news broke, it sent shock waves through the industry: The model we had relied on, the very structure that had propelled our business to incredible heights, was being dismantled, removing our sales teams and changing the model to move straight to affiliate sales. This

THE MULTIPLY METHOD

meant we would lose over 99 percent of our income as we lost our sales teams. The business I had poured my heart and soul into was gone—*overnight*.

In an instant, everything I had built seemed to vanish. I found myself standing at a crossroads, uncertain of what would come next. My mind raced, replaying the journey I had just completed. It wasn't just loss of opportunity, but also loss of community. *Could we do it again?*

At the time, I was still actively coaching within my community, the Network Marketing Inner Circle. The sales strategies and systems we had developed were delivering real results, and entrepreneurs from all walks of life were celebrating their wins week after week. We were seeing success stories unfold constantly as people implemented our systems and transformed their businesses. We were also sharing our Multiply Method with leaders from other companies through our Made to Multiply Mastermind, helping them scale their teams and reach new heights. But despite all the momentum and progress happening around me, I couldn't help but wonder . . . *what about me?*

Could these same systems work for us again? Could we replicate the success we had built? I knew the systems worked. But would they work as powerfully the second time around, when the stakes were higher? I had only one shot if I were to do it again, as I didn't want to dilute my network or my credibility in the industry. I couldn't let anyone down. This left me teetering between doubling down on coaching or continuing to coach while also

AN OVERVIEW OF THE MULTIPLY METHOD

starting a new company and building a brand-new team.

As I looked around at the team I had mentored, the families we had helped, the lives we had changed, one question kept echoing in my mind: *What now?*

But here's the thing about entrepreneurship, and particularly the network marketing industry: It's not only about the product or the pay plan. It's always been about the *people*—the relationships, the leadership, and the systems that empower others to succeed. And as much as I had lost, I hadn't lost the one thing that truly mattered: *community.*

I started to think, *How sad would it be NOT to do it again?*

I knew, without a doubt, that I wasn't done. We had many more lives to change.

In that moment of uncertainty, a sense of clarity washed over me. I didn't just want to rebuild a team. I wanted to *reinvent* it—faster, smarter, and stronger than before. I had seen firsthand how the network marketing model could transform lives—not just financially, but on a deeper, more personal level. I believed in it. Despite all that had happened to me, I still believed in *this* model. And I knew that if I could leverage the lessons learned, the proven systems I had created—the Multiply Method—there was nothing standing in the way of building something even greater.

That's when I made the decision.

I would start again. But this time, I wasn't starting from scratch. I was starting with experience, wisdom, and a proven system that had already changed the lives of hundreds of thousands. And I wasn't doing it alone. I would build an amazing team again. Together, we would prove that the Multiply Method wasn't just a one-time success; it was a system that would stand the test of time.

The Multiply Method was ready to be birthed prior to the "bad news," but we hadn't set a publishing date yet. I knew there must be more to share and another chapter to be written. In a way, the delay in writing this book was a blessing. It was a chance for me to see if the Multiply Method could stand up to the challenge of reinvention. And the results? Well, they've been nothing short of extraordinary. During the last day leading in my previous company, I hit the top of the plan in our new company during my first full month in business.

I'll be the first to admit, it hasn't been easy. Building a team from scratch, especially after the loss of something so monumental, is never easy, even when you already have experience and systems in place. But what I've learned, and what has been reinforced, is this: *The principles that work in network marketing—the ones that result in true, lasting success—don't change.* The systems that produce results aren't dependent on the company. They aren't reliant on some magical compensation plan. They are rooted in leadership, strategy, and authentic relationships with people who are driven to succeed.

And now we are doing it again.

We are doing it *faster* than the first time.

AN OVERVIEW OF THE MULTIPLY METHOD

We are not starting over; we are building on the foundation of years of experience and knowledge. This time, the team is expanding faster than ever before—*because we're not just teaching people how to make money; we're teaching them how to multiply their success.*

> **WE'RE NOT JUST TEACHING PEOPLE HOW TO MAKE MONEY; WE'RE TEACHING THEM HOW TO MULTIPLY THEIR SUCCESS.**

This book is the result of that journey. It's a road map for anyone who wants to achieve the same level of success, no matter where you're starting from. Whether you're new to network marketing or you've been in the industry for years, the Multiply Method is designed to simplify the process of building a team, generating sales, and creating lasting success through duplication.

In the following chapters, I'll break down the exact steps we've used to build one of the fastest-growing sales teams in history. I'll show you the strategies, systems, and mindset shifts that have led to over $2 billion in annual sales. I'll explain how we've been able to create a movement that's not just changing the lives of those in the business, but also leaving a lasting impact on their families, communities, and the world at large. To me, this book and sharing my systems with others are about leaving a legacy.

Whether you're in the beginning stages of your journey or you're looking to take your existing business to the next level, I invite you to follow along. You don't have to reinvent the wheel. You just have to multiply what's already working.

Let's MULTIPLY!

How This All Started

It was 2008, the height of the recession. I was a shy, young kindergarten teacher in my twenties. I lived in Motown—Detroit, the heart of the American automotive industry—and the city was struggling. The auto industry had all but collapsed, leaving thousands of people without jobs. Homes were being foreclosed, and schools were closing. In the midst of all this, I was doing what I had always dreamed of: teaching. But my dream job came with its own set of challenges.

Though I was the most requested teacher in my building, I quickly learned that in the world of education, tenure often trumps performance. Because I was the low person on the totem pole, my job would be the first to

AN OVERVIEW OF THE MULTIPLY METHOD

go, and everyone knew it. I remember walking into the teachers' lounge every day. The whispers would start, heads would turn, and I'd be greeted with the same questions: "How are you feeling?" "What will you do next?" I had no answers. My stomach would churn, and soon I couldn't bear to hear those words anymore. Eventually, I stopped going to the teachers' lounge altogether and ate lunch in my car, just to avoid the uncomfortable conversations.

It was an unsettling time. What would I do if I lost my job? What would happen next?

Teaching had always been my dream job. As a child, I used to line up my dolls and teach them school. As a teen, I ran summer babysitting camps, charging parents for childcare and teaching the kids how to read and write. Teaching was in my blood. But when the economy crashed, it felt like the dream I'd built my whole life around was in jeopardy. It wasn't just about the job security anymore; it was about something deeper—the pressure to provide for my family and create a future that felt stable and secure.

Pressure Promotes You

They say that pressure either breaks you or promotes you. I chose to let it promote me.

I had no choice but to look for extra work. My finances were becoming increasingly tight. There were budget cuts everywhere, and with a classroom budget of just $100 a year, I had to buy my own supplies. So I prayed for extra earning opportunities, hoping for a way out.

Then one day, my mother called me with an opportunity that would change the course of my life forever. She had been freelancing for different skincare and cosmetic companies and was making twenty dollars an hour. She helped me get a job doing the same thing.

> **THEY SAY THAT PRESSURE EITHER BREAKS YOU OR PROMOTES YOU. I CHOSE TO LET IT PROMOTE ME.**

One of the companies she introduced me to was the company where I got my start in direct sales. At the time, they were primarily a retail business but were looking to shift into the social selling model. I didn't know anything about social selling, and honestly, I had always told myself I would *never* do it. I had heard the stereotypes, wasn't into sales myself, and thought the whole thing wasn't for me.

But my mother, Kris, a savvy entrepreneur, encouraged me. She said, "I know the possibilities here. We'd be

AN OVERVIEW OF THE MULTIPLY METHOD

crazy not to do this."

As a firstborn child, I tend to be the compliant one, so I listened to her. I said yes. And that yes led me down a path I could never have imagined. I started working my network marketing business part-time, alongside my full-time teaching job. That first year, I made enough to supplement my income. But by the end of the second year, I had replaced my full-time salary entirely. I decided to put in my leave of absence from my teaching job and just never went back. And now . . . I've never looked back!

**From Humble Beginnings
to a Billion-Dollar Brand**
When I started my network marketing business, we had no systems, no upline support, and no training. I was alone, navigating the waters of a new business model with little to guide me. But I had something else going for me: an intense desire to succeed. I dove into learning. I attended industry events, read books, invested heavily in mentors and masterminds, and studied everything I could find on building a successful network marketing business.

I quickly realized that success in this industry wasn't about luck or chance—it was about systems. And so, I began to create my own.

The result? A system that would help build one of the fastest-growing sales teams in network marketing

THE MULTIPLY METHOD

history. We did in five years what it takes most companies fifty years to achieve. A billion dollars in sales per year. Yes, you read that right. *A billion dollars.*

Some would call that a "unicorn brand." But to me, it wasn't about the profit. It was about the people. It wasn't about the revenue. It was about the relationships. We created a sales team of hundreds of thousands who served millions of customers. This was about creating a team of incredible individuals who didn't just want to make money—they wanted to change their lives, their communities, and the world around them.

Because of our success I started to get asked by others: "Do you offer coaching?" We started our coaching program, the Network Marketing Inner Circle, for those who wanted to achieve their first six-figure year, and our leadership mastermind, Made to Multiply, for those who wanted to scale from six-figure years to six-figure months! Companies started asking us to consult and keynote, and we began seeing leaders all across our profession succeed with our systems.

The Multiply Method became the backbone of our success. It was the system that made everything possible, a system that helped people from different companies—with different products and pay plans—become more profitable.

Our systems turn businesses into billion-dollar brands.

AN OVERVIEW OF THE MULTIPLY METHOD

What Is the Multiply Method?

The Multiply Method is a set of simple yet powerful systems designed to help anyone build a successful network marketing business, regardless of experience. The system revolves around several key principles, each designed to maximize results and minimize complexity. These systems have helped thousands of entrepreneurs across the globe achieve financial freedom and build massive teams.

Why Systems Are Key to Success in Social Selling
I've often compared network marketing to *pseudo-franchising*—a model where each person operates like a mini-franchisee. Each distributor is responsible for their own business, selling products and building teams, but they don't have to deal with the overhead costs associated with traditional businesses. There are no employees to manage, no brick-and-mortar locations to rent, and no hefty startup fees. Pretty smart model, right? It's one of the only models where you can be profitable right away, with little cost and really no risk.

Imagine this: A local coffee shop in a rural town makes the best coffee in the world, but the owner refuses to franchise. They keep it small, never expanding, never replicating. The business is successful, but it's limited. That's what happens when a business model lacks the ability to scale.

Now imagine another coffee shop that franchises. It's well known, and you can find a location on nearly every street corner. The business model has been replicated time and time again, and as a result, it's become a billion-dollar brand. That's the power of systems. Just like the franchise model, network marketing thrives on replicating simple systems that anyone can follow. But it's actually simpler—and easier to scale.

The Power of Replicating Systems
Think about a company such as Starbucks—it's everywhere, right? No matter where you go, you can find a Starbucks. Whether you're in a bustling city or a small suburban town, you know exactly what to expect when you walk in. You don't have to wonder if the coffee will taste the same, or if the service will be up to par. That's because Starbucks operates on a simple, replicable system. Each store follows the same set of procedures, ensuring a consistent customer experience no matter where you are.

This is the power of a *replicating* business model—it's the secret sauce that allows companies to scale quickly and effectively. Franchises aren't just about selling a product; they're about selling a system. And that system is what makes it possible for one person to replicate the success of another, time and time again. Whether it's the way the barista prepares your coffee, the way the store is laid out, or the way the company trains its employees, every aspect is designed to be *replicable* and *scalable*.

Now let's relate that to network marketing. Our business model is essentially pseudo-franchising, but

AN OVERVIEW OF THE MULTIPLY METHOD

without the overhead. In traditional franchising, each location must be staffed with employees, have a physical store, and manage various operational costs. In network marketing, you don't need to worry about all of that. Instead, you have *individual franchisees*—each distributor working from their own home and building their own business, but following a common system that guarantees their success.

> **IT'S NOT ABOUT YOUR PERSONAL SKILLS, YOUR CHARISMA, OR THE NUMBER OF PEOPLE YOU KNOW. IT'S ABOUT THE SYSTEM.**

This is why systems are so powerful in network marketing. Just like Starbucks, you don't need to reinvent the wheel every time you bring someone new onto your team. The key is to give them a simple, effective system that they can plug into and duplicate. That's how you scale quickly. It's not about your personal skills, your charisma,

THE MULTIPLY METHOD

or the number of people you know. It's about the system. The simpler the system, the faster it builds.

The beauty of network marketing is that, much like a franchise, once you've perfected your systems, you can grow exponentially. When people follow the same steps, they can achieve similar results. That's why I like to say that *success leaves clues*. When you build a simple system that anyone can follow, you create a business that can grow and multiply with little to no extra effort on your part. This is the magic of *duplication*, and it's the reason network marketing is one of the most powerful business models in the world.

> **WHEN YOU BUILD A SIMPLE SYSTEM THAT ANYONE CAN FOLLOW, YOU CREATE A BUSINESS THAT CAN GROW AND MULTIPLY WITH LITTLE TO NO EXTRA EFFORT ON YOUR PART. THIS IS THE MAGIC OF *DUPLICATION*.**

AN OVERVIEW OF THE MULTIPLY METHOD

The Key to Momentum: Keep It Simple
The fastest-growing sales teams in network marketing focus on simplicity. They understand that momentum is built by many people doing a little bit—and doing it consistently. The simpler the system, the faster the growth.

> MOMENTUM IS BUILT BY MANY PEOPLE DOING A LITTLE BIT— AND DOING IT CONSISTENTLY.

> THE SIMPLER THE SYSTEM, THE FASTER THE GROWTH.

That's where the Multiply Method comes in.

The Multiply Method is designed to help people duplicate success quickly by following a straightforward system that works for anybody, in any company, in direct sales.

The Multiply Method: Simple Systems for Building a Solid, Sustainable Network Marketing Team

The Multiply Method is made up of simple, replicable systems designed to help you build a successful, sustainable network marketing business. Each step in this process is essential to creating lasting momentum and achieving long-term success. Let's break down the key systems that will help you build and scale your business.

1. Prospecting: The Art of Inviting

Prospecting is the process of inviting people into your business. This step is about learning where to find people who could become potential customers or business partners and what to say to them to start a conversation.

When I started my business, I was shy and had no network to speak of. But I created a prospecting system that helped me become the number one recruiter in my company. I want you to understand that success in this business isn't about your personality or your existing network. It's about plugging into a system for prospecting that anyone can use to find leads. With the Multiply Method, you'll learn exactly where to find prospects, and you'll discover the "words that work" to start a conversation.

AN OVERVIEW OF THE MULTIPLY METHOD

> **SUCCESS IN THIS BUSINESS ISN'T ABOUT YOUR PERSONALITY OR YOUR EXISTING NETWORK. IT'S ABOUT PLUGGING INTO A SYSTEM FOR PROSPECTING THAT ANYONE CAN USE TO FIND LEADS.**

2. Presenting: Turning Interest into Opportunity

Once you have someone interested in learning more, *presenting* your product or opportunity is the next critical step. This is where most people complicate things. You don't need scripts or spammy sales tactics. What you need are *authentic, powerful conversations* that present your opportunity in a clear and professional way.

By simplifying the process and making it something anyone on your team can replicate, you'll see more people having success with the presentation. This is exactly how I became the top closer in my company and developed several successful teams within our organization. Keep it simple—everyone should be able to duplicate your approach.

3. Closing: Conquering Objections and Sealing the Deal

Now comes the art of *closing*—getting people through your prospecting funnel and into your business. It's one thing to get someone's attention, but getting them to say yes is where the magic happens. Closing involves overcoming objections and guiding your prospect to make a decision—whether that's as a *customer, consultant* (business partner), or *connector* (someone who refers others).

I believe everyone can successfully plug in as one of the 3 Cs: customer, consultant, or connector. The key to mastering this step is understanding the simple system that helps you close effectively and confidently.

4. Fast Start: Launching Your New Team Members to Success

Now that you've recruited someone into your business, what's next? How do you get them off to the best possible start? This is where I often see people get stuck. As a former teacher, I love creating easy-to-follow, step-by-step systems. That's why I excel at the Fast Start system.

When I am introduced at industry events, the person introducing me always says that I have developed more top leaders direct to me than almost anyone else

AN OVERVIEW OF THE MULTIPLY METHOD

in my industry. Most top leaders have one or two power legs or leaders. I'm proud to say that I've personally sponsored and mentored fifteen top leaders directly, with more than fifty people personally enrolled who are consistently ranking up at any given time. The Fast Start system is the secret to getting people launched with success from day one, keeping it simple, and watching them soar.

5. Customer Acquisition:
Building a Strong, Customer-Centric Business

The majority of the billions of dollars in sales in our organization come from customers, not recruits. This is the true sign of a healthy organization. Building a customer base is essential for sustainable growth. Our customer acquisition system focuses on attracting, engaging, and retaining customers who are genuinely excited about the products and results.

Fun fact: The majority of our top team members started as customers! Your goal is to build an army of loyal customers who are thrilled with their results—and who stick around for the long haul.

6. Customer Retention:
Keeping Them Coming Back for More

It's one thing to get a customer, but it's another to keep them. Building a business that thrives means having a customer retention system that encourages regular orders, reorders, referrals, upsells, and even upgrades when people join you in the business. We've developed a system that ensures that customers keep coming back for more—and it's what supports the long-term health of a business.

Our system focuses on making sure that your customers are not just one-time buyers, but lifelong advocates who continue to see value in your products, month after month.

7. Events: Accelerating Your Growth Through Experiences

Events are a powerful way to exponentially grow your business. Whether virtual or in person, events allow you to showcase your product, your opportunity, and your community in a way that words alone can't do. Events are *experiential*—they create an environment where people feel connected, inspired, and motivated to take action. They not only highlight the opportunity but allow people to experience the community.

We've developed a simple system for events that walks you through the entire process—from planning to execution—ensuring that your events are always impactful and will help you move your business forward.

8. Social Media: Letting Your Ideal Clients Find You

The power of social media cannot be overstated. All of my leads come to me *organically*—without my paying for ads—because people have found me through my content or social media interactions. My simple strategy for selling more and sponsoring more on social media results in your ideal clients coming to *you*.

AN OVERVIEW OF THE MULTIPLY METHOD

The best part? You'll never run out of leads when you master social media. It's an endless resource of qualified prospects, and when you know how to use it effectively, it becomes a gold mine for your business.

9. Leadership Development:
Creating Leaders Who Multiply

Leadership development is the real "gold" of network marketing. This is the part of the business that people rarely teach, but it's the part that will transform your organization. My Made to Multiply Mastermind clients go on a journey together and learn how to develop leaders quickly and effectively. The systems we use are advanced, but they allow you to duplicate leadership in record time.

If you want to become a leader, or if you want to develop new leaders in your team, this is where you'll get the edge. I'll show you how to build a leadership system that is *efficient* and *scalable*—and it's one that also *duplicates*.

10. Team Training + Communication:
Building a Culture of Duplication

Culture is the glue that holds your team together. Without strong communication and a unified culture, your team will struggle to duplicate success. That's why we've created a system for team training and communication that drives duplication.

By having a strong, consistent training system in place, everyone on your team can plug in and duplicate your success. When you've created a culture of empowerment and consistency, you'll see your business grow rapidly. And the best part? It will be stress-free.

These systems are the backbone of the Multiply Method, which is made up of simple, successful, and scalable systems that anyone can follow to build a thriving network marketing business. As you plug into these systems, you'll find that success isn't about doing everything yourself; it's about creating a system that works and getting others to replicate it.

Why Network Marketing? And Why Now?

I believe network marketing is the best business model on the planet. It's a low-risk, high-reward opportunity that requires very little up-front investment. In fact, in many cases, you can start a business with less than a hundred dollars. It's the great equalizer—where success doesn't depend on your background, your education, or your social network. It depends on your ability to follow a proven system.

If you're ready to step into a future where you can live more, give more, and love your life more, then network marketing is the path for you. This business model gives you the freedom to design your life on your terms and the potential to create a business that generates real, lasting success. I want to give you the systems to soar and build the sales team of your dreams.

AN OVERVIEW OF THE MULTIPLY METHOD

> **IT'S THE GREAT EQUALIZER—WHERE SUCCESS DOESN'T DEPEND ON YOUR BACKGROUND, YOUR EDUCATION, OR YOUR SOCIAL NETWORK. IT DEPENDS ON YOUR ABILITY TO FOLLOW A PROVEN SYSTEM.**

Conclusion

As you read through *The Multiply Method* and put the systems into practice, I want you to remember why you're doing this. Your WHY is the fuel that drives your success. When you get clear on your vision and commit to the journey, the sky's the limit.

In the next chapters, we will dive deeper into the systems that will help you grow a successful business, create a thriving team, and build a legacy you can be proud of.

Your dreams are within reach—let's make them happen together!

THE MULTIPLY METHOD

Application

Write your WHY. As you do, consider this question: *If time and money were no object, what would your life look like?* Use this prompt to help you define why you are building your business.

_____

_____

_____

_____

_____

_____

_____

_____

_____

CHAPTER 1

PROSPECTING (THE ART OF INVITING): WHO TO INVITE AND HOW

WHEN I FIRST began my network marketing business, I was far from a confident, outgoing entrepreneur. I was a shy, young schoolteacher with no network to speak of, no experience in sales, and no idea where to begin. But I knew one thing: If I wanted to be successful in this business, I would have to be a student of our profession and learn the art of inviting or, as we call it in the industry, *prospecting*.

Prospecting—the act of reaching out, initiating conversations, inviting others, and building connections—is at the heart of network marketing. To grow your business, you need to learn how to start and nurture relationships with new people, and you need to embrace the power of networking. But what does it take to be successful at this? And who exactly should you be inviting?

> **TO GROW YOUR BUSINESS, YOU NEED TO LEARN HOW TO START AND NURTURE RELATIONSHIPS WITH NEW PEOPLE, AND YOU NEED TO EMBRACE THE POWER OF NETWORKING.**

Through years of trial and error, I've discovered the core principles that top network marketers follow when prospecting. Today, I want to share these with you. This simple, repeatable system allows you to connect with people and grow your business without feeling "sales-y."

The One Thing Top Earners Have in Common

Over the years, I've had the privilege of attending numerous industry events where top earners from different companies are interviewed on stage. Despite working with different products and compensation

PROSPECTING (THE ART OF INVITING): WHO TO INVITE AND HOW

plans, there's always one thing they have in common. *They are all great prospectors.*

Every year, top leaders are brought on stage and asked a series of questions to prove this commonality:

How long have you been in your business?
The responses range from five to more than thirty-five years!

How many conversations or presentations have you had for your business?
The responses range from hundreds to thousands!

How many people have you personally sponsored as a result?
The numbers range from fifty to over two hundred fifty, over time.

How many people do the majority of your sales come from?
Usually it's one to three leadership legs or leaders. That's it.

Although they had entirely different backgrounds and came from different companies with different compensation plans, they all had one thing in common: *They were all great prospectors!* They'd had many conversations and made many great connections for their business—which ultimately led them to find a handful of people who built tremendous sales teams.

And that's what prospecting is all about—talking

to more people about your opportunity or product and making authentic connections. And when you prioritize people over product—and relationship over revenue—you will not only be the person whom people want to do business with, you will also be the person they want to refer other people to.

> WHEN YOU PRIORITIZE PEOPLE OVER PRODUCT—AND RELATIONSHIP OVER REVENUE—YOU WILL NOT ONLY BE THE PERSON WHOM PEOPLE WANT TO DO BUSINESS WITH, YOU WILL ALSO BE THE PERSON THEY WANT TO REFER OTHER PEOPLE TO.

PROSPECTING (THE ART OF INVITING): WHO TO INVITE AND HOW

Over the years, the characteristic I discovered most successful entrepreneurs—and not just the ones in our industry—have is that they are great conversationalists. Good networkers are good at networking! They are good at paying compliments and then transitioning into conversation by asking questions and being genuinely interested in other people.

Think about it: The number one thing that people love to talk about is themselves! And it's really easy to ask others questions.

This is how I became great at prospecting.

I am going to share with you my simple system for prospecting that works effectively in every setting. It doesn't require spammy scripts or sliding into DMs to bug your best friend. It's the simple art of inviting!

The Power of Connecting with People

When I say *prospecting*, I'm not talking about sending cold, impersonal messages or making a sales pitch to strangers. Prospecting is about making connections and starting conversations. It's about prioritizing the person in front of you over the product or opportunity you want to sell. And when you focus on the person, not the product, people will not only want to do business with you—they'll want to refer others to you as well.

I want to share with you the system I've used to become great at prospecting. This system has allowed me to build relationships with people both online and offline, without being pushy and without resorting to spammy sales tactics.

The Simple System: Compliment → Conversation → Connection

Let's break down my proven system for prospecting into three simple steps:

1. **Compliment**
2. **Conversation**
3. **Connection**

It really is that simple! Let's dive deeper into each step so you can start using this system today.

Reaching Out to People You Know

Before I share my system for conversation, I want you to understand what *not* to do when reaching out.

I remember during the peak of the pandemic, someone reached out and asked me, "Would you like to order my product and help me achieve a sales goal?" I always love giving people the benefit of the doubt, so I thought, *I'm sure she's excited about her business, but I just had a baby. We haven't connected in a long time. I wish we could have made a personal connection first!*

PROSPECTING (THE ART OF INVITING): WHO TO INVITE AND HOW

Let me preface what I'm about to share with this: I train social sellers how to build successful businesses. I understood my friend's intentions. I knew her heart. She was super excited to share her product with me! So I responded back thoughtfully: "What if I could share a better way to help you get the best response from people you are reaching out to and reconnecting with?"

You see, we hadn't spoken in a while, and if I had been another person on the receiving end who wasn't in our industry—and didn't understand her heart or motives—I could have easily been offended that she hadn't made a personal connection and attempted to rekindle our relationship or engaged in any type of conversation first.

The good news is, there is a better way.

Write this down: *Compliment → Conversation → Connection*

Let's dive into the details.

Before we talk about how to start conversations with people, let's first talk about who to reach out to. Building a network starts with the people you already know. When I first got started, I made a list of everyone I knew, who included:

- Friends
- Family
- Their friends and family
- Professional contacts
- People in my social groups
- Social media contacts

THE MULTIPLY METHOD

I then brought them through my prospecting process, which starts with a compliment or congratulations to rekindle the conversation. I continue by asking lots of questions. And then I make the connection about my business!

Step 1: Compliment
When reaching out, start with something positive. If you haven't been connected to someone for some time, I recommend scrolling through their social media to find their most recent news or an exciting event in their life and then offering them a compliment or congratulations.

Compliments or congratulations go a long way in helping you reconnect with people. But they must be *genuine*. If someone posts about a life event, a new project, or a success, this is a great way to get the conversation going. You could comment on a recent trip they took, a personal achievement they had, or even a cute pet or an addition to their family.

Example message: *Hey, [Name], congratulations on your recent promotion! I saw the news on social media and I'm so excited for you! I know it's been a while, and I wanted to reconnect. How are you doing?*

Step 2: Conversation
After giving the compliment or congratulations, ask them open-ended questions to begin a conversation. People love to talk about themselves, so give them the space to

PROSPECTING (THE ART OF INVITING): WHO TO INVITE AND HOW

share. Think of it this way: You are simply reconnecting and getting caught up. That should take the pressure off!

Example questions: *How are you and your family doing? What's been the most exciting thing in your life lately?*

The goal here is to be genuinely interested in their life. Don't rush to turn the conversation into a sales pitch. Just listen, engage, and be curious. Focus on having a good conversation.

> **DON'T RUSH TO TURN THE CONVERSATION INTO A SALES PITCH. JUST LISTEN, ENGAGE, AND BE CURIOUS. FOCUS ON HAVING A GOOD CONVERSATION.**

Step 3: Connection

Eventually, after you've built rapport, you'll want to connect the conversation to your business when the time feels right. It may be after a few messages—or after a few days. Don't force it—wait for the right moment. Once you've reconnected and have had some good conversation, share what you're working on, especially if it aligns with their interests. But don't make the focus all about you. Make it about how you can help them or how your business might be of interest to them or someone they know. Ask for their opinion or help as you expand.

Example message: *I noticed you're in [location]. That area is actually one of the places I'm focusing on expanding my business. Have you heard of [company/product]? I'd love to get your thoughts on it. And if nothing else, it would be great to catch up! Would you want to meet up for [virtual] coffee? My treat!*

You're not pitching. You're just making a connection. The goal is to get them on the phone, reconnect with them, and rekindle the relationship. Have a deeper conversation and see where things go from there. I like to share my excitement for what I'm doing, too, in hopes that they may know people who may be interested, or perhaps they may have interest themselves. (We will share more about what to say during these conversations in the next chapter.)

This approach is a great way to reconnect with people you know—and even to get referrals for your business.

Reaching Out to People You Don't Know

So, what about connecting with people you don't know? It's a similar system. It just requires a little more effort in finding opportunities to meet new individuals.

PROSPECTING (THE ART OF INVITING): WHO TO INVITE AND HOW

I personally love using *samples* when prospecting, but if your company doesn't offer samples, you can still have conversations with people and then connect on social media.

The three-step system still applies:

- **Compliment:** Compliment something about them or their service.
- **Conversation:** Start a conversation with a genuine question. Stay engaged by asking questions.
- **Connection:** After having a great conversation, offer a sample and/or connect on social media.

For example, imagine you're at a store and you meet a salesclerk who's providing excellent service. Here's how you might use the system:

- **Compliment:** "Thanks for the great service today! You've been so helpful!"
- **Conversation**: "Do you enjoy what you do? Is this full-time work for you?" Continue the conversation.
- **Connection:** After we have a good conversation, I make the connection to my business by providing a sample or connecting on social media. If I have a sample with me, I'll say, "I've loved chatting with you today. I'd like to leave you with a gift. Have you heard of _____ before? This is my company. You're going to

love this [tell more about it]. If you promise me you'll use it, I promise you I'll follow up and stay in touch! Are you on social?" (Then connect there for follow-up!)

If I do not have a sample, I immediately connect on social. At the end of our conversation, I pull out my phone and say, "I've loved chatting with you today. I'd like to stay in touch. Are you on social?" Then, I connect with them there and follow up!

Let's Review

When you're prospecting (talking to people), the goal is to make the conversation about them—not you! Think TINY: *Their Interest, Not Yours!*

Compliment/Congratulate
Say something nice to make a connection. "Hey, Amy, you and your family have been on my mind. Congrats on the move! How are you doing?"

Conversation
Have genuine conversation—be genuinely interested in the other person and ask a lot of questions.

Connection
At a natural point in the conversation, you can make a connection: "I see you're in Utah now. I have a business

PROSPECTING (THE ART OF INVITING): WHO TO INVITE AND HOW

that's expanding there. Have you heard of _____ before? I'd love to share it—and get your feedback on growing there. If nothing else, let's get caught up!"

Set a time to connect. Offer to meet them and treat them to coffee (or invite them to virtual coffee).

We will share how to present the business in the next chapter.

There are many great places where you can find prospects for your business. Now that we know *how*, let's talk about *who*.

Ways to Meet More Prospects

Outside of reconnecting with people you know and making new connections in person, there are plenty of opportunities to meet prospects for your business. Here are some ideas:

Events

I will share my simple system for successful events in an upcoming chapter. Events are a great way to maximize your time and get your company in front of a lot of people at once. You can do these locally or virtually, or even do both simultaneously. Events were the single most powerful thing we did to grow our business fast. Whether or not your company has an events plan or host incentives, I think everyone should implement events, especially for community-based businesses that have many products that are experiential.

THE MULTIPLY METHOD

> EVENTS WERE THE SINGLE MOST POWERFUL THING WE DID TO GROW OUR BUSINESS FAST.

Networking Groups
Whether they're in person or online, networking groups are a great way to build connections with other professionals. Networking relationships tend to be "give to get," so you'll want to be consistent in offering value to other people as you spend time building these relationships. I love teaching this to my Inner Circle coaching clients. You can search for networking groups in your area, and you can also network in online groups. The key with any type of networking group is discovering how you can give value to others, whether it's through referrals or recommendations or even providing value in conversations. These relationships are very reciprocal in nature. Ask, "How can I best support you in business?" and expect that they will do the same. Keep showing up for one another!

PROSPECTING (THE ART OF INVITING): WHO TO INVITE AND HOW

Vendor Events and Trade Shows

Vendor events are another great way to meet new people. Not only are you surrounded by new people, you are also surrounded by other hardworking entrepreneurs who are hosting space at the events. I love going early to set up and meet all the vendors—and show interest in their business. I also love to stay late and exchange contact information so I can connect with others later and discuss how we can help one another grow. I had several top leaders join me after I met them at these types of events!

I look at vendor events and trade shows as a great way to build my list and expand my network. To build my list, I always have a raffle or giveaway to pull people in: "Come enter to win!" On the entry form, I create space for their name and contact info. I also like to ask a specific question on the form: "If you could change one thing about your _____ what would it be?"

(For example, if you sell skincare, ask: "If you could change one thing about your skin, what would it be?")

Then, I show them the suggested solution, make a recommendation based on their response, and ask if they'd like to give it a try! Raffles are a great tool for follow-up. For everyone who didn't win the raffle, tell them about your specials and the solutions you recommend, and then ask if they'd like to give it a try. Add their names and contact info to your follow-up list for future newsletters, specials, or events that may interest them.

THE MULTIPLY METHOD

Professionals
You can find people in your niche by searching professional sites such as LinkedIn or in other online groups. Let's say your business is skincare and you want to find other aestheticians (people in the skincare business) who would be great candidates for what you do. If you're in nutrition, you might search for personal trainers or nutritionists. You can connect by vocation or even location (search for entrepreneurs in your area). The key to connecting with professionals is to find commonality and a reason to connect.

Commonality: "I see you're in the skincare business!" or "I see you're a small business owner in our area!"

Connection: "I'm looking to network with other people in our profession! Tell me more about yourself." Then, continue the conversation: "I'd love to meet up for coffee [or virtual coffee] and see how we can help each other expand!"

I remember a business owner who reached out to me using a similar approach. Kathleen owned a cookie shop. She introduced herself to me by saying, "I see you're a small business owner in the area. I am too. Could we meet for coffee and see how we can connect on ways to help one another grow?" When we sat down together for coffee, I learned all about her cookie shop. I suggested her cookies would make great gifts for our ladies in business. Next, I explained my WHY, WHAT we do, and WHO we were looking for (people to try our

PROSPECTING (THE ART OF INVITING): WHO TO INVITE AND HOW

products, as well as people to promote them). When I asked Kathleen, "Who do you know that these products may be great for?" she said, "Me!" And then she joined me in business!

Social Media
Social media is a great way to meet new people. In fact, it's how I generate most of my leads. It's also why I spend the most time coaching my Inner Circle clients on the latest ways to generate leads online. Although social media is changing all the time (which is why we can't get too detailed on specific platforms in the book), I will share some high-level strategies on social in a later chapter. You can also find the latest strategies in our Network Marketing Inner Circle coaching community.

The Ultimate Goal in Prospecting Is to Make New Friends!

I met one of my best leaders on the beaches of Bora Bora by focusing on forming a friendship. I was on a company trip, lying by the pool, when I noticed a couple sitting next to me. I paid them a compliment and started a conversation. I asked a lot of questions, showing genuine interest in getting to know them. I learned she was the reigning Mrs. Hawaii and had a background in nutrition. They were a military family who moved around a lot with their young children. I made the conversation all about

THE MULTIPLY METHOD

her, which led her to being naturally curious about me. She later told the story that she was curious because I didn't share much about myself! I talked less about me, and more about her, and we later connected on social.

Did you notice that? *Compliment. Conversation. Connection.*

When we connected on social, she did some snooping on her own. Turns out, she was intrigued by what I did! She ended up recruiting herself to my network marketing business, explaining that she'd like to learn more. She later became one of our top leaders and a very good friend. All because we had first built a relationship!

Most Successful Leaders Are Great Networkers

We have it backward when we make it all about us! Since I started my business, I have had thousands of conversations and made hundreds of presentations to recruit a few hundred people—and a few of my sales teams went on to sell to millions of customers and produce billions of dollars in sales in a year!

Prospecting is all about finding the few who will "do"! As I shared in my first book, *Rock Your Network Marketing Business*, you never know what people will do—or who they will lead you to.

PROSPECTING (THE ART OF INVITING): WHO TO INVITE AND HOW

PROSPECTING IS ALL ABOUT FINDING THE FEW WHO WILL "DO"!

The Story of the Fifty Million Dollar Woman

Even if you've already heard this story, it's worth repeating, as it's one of the most powerful stories on prospecting. It's why every conversation counts. You never know what someone will do—or who they could lead you to.

One of my first business partners wasn't willing to do much to share about their business, and eventually decided she wanted to quit. Upon her request to exit, I asked her to give one more conversation a try. I asked if I wrote an email to her contacts, would she be willing to send it to her network? She said yes; I helped her draft it and off it went.

One of her connections read it and said, "I'm interested." After a short conversation with me, she said, "I'm in!" This happened on New Year's Eve—what a toast to new beginnings!

My business partner couldn't get over the fact that she'd worked *that hard* to find one person. But I did my best to encourage her, saying, "You never know what that one person could do, or who they could lead you to." Despite this, she eventually quit. However, her business

THE MULTIPLY METHOD

partner—who joined because of that email—went on to build one of the most successful sales teams in the company, one that we estimate with conservative growth would reach $50 million in lifetime earnings. That was a costly mistake on my business partner's part.

I'm not one to judge, as I've made costly mistakes too.

Write this down: *Passive prospecting can be your greatest mistake.*

Have you ever assumed that your ideal prospect would reach out to *you* if they were interested? I made this mistake, and I learned a really expensive lesson from it: If you think someone is great, someone else does too. And somebody *will* reach out to them. So why not now, and why not you?

Stacey was on my dream team list. I worked for her—she was one of the most networked, accomplished women I knew! But because I didn't want to interrupt her life or mess up our friendship, I made the mistake of assuming she would reach out to me if she was interested in my network marketing business. And so I would passively post on Facebook and pray that Stacey would see my posts and contact me. Big mistake!

Rose also thought Stacey would be great, and she reached out to her, using the system that I shared earlier. She complimented her: "Stacey, I know you've built a great network in Chicago. I'm building a business there!" And then they started a conversation, with Rose making the connection: "I'd love to treat you to coffee and get your input—and see if you know anyone who may be interested in my network marketing business!"

PROSPECTING (THE ART OF INVITING): WHO TO INVITE AND HOW

When she met Rose for coffee, Stacey had a list of hundreds of referrals that she was ready to share. When Rose explained what she was up to, Stacey insisted on learning more for herself. Rose invited her to a special event with a guest speaker—and who do you think was the guest speaker that night? Yours truly! To my surprise, Stacey joined that night and became the company's number one recruiter that year.

Now I always ask myself, *Which is greater—the risk or the reward?*

What is the worst that will happen? They say no. You won't die. I have yet to die reaching out to people about my business. It's not personal rejection. It's personal preference.

And what if your dream comes true? The person you reached out to joins you—and they end up being your top team builder.

Be purposeful with your prospecting. You never know what people will do. Or who they will lead you to. It's your job to share; it's theirs to decide.

IT'S YOUR JOB TO SHARE; IT'S THEIRS TO DECIDE.

So what do you say to people when you connect with your ideal client? Like Rose did when she sat down with Stacey. . . .More on that in the next chapter!

THE MULTIPLY METHOD

Application

Write down the names of the individuals who are on your top-five "dream team" list. Scroll social and find one thing you can compliment each person on; then start a conversation by reaching out and asking them some questions.

Name	What can you compliment this person on?

CHAPTER 2

PRESENTING: SHARING YOUR BUSINESS POWERFULLY AND PROFESSIONALLY

I REMEMBER THE first time I shared my business with another person. As I approached a woman at a cosmetics counter, my hands were shaking, my knees were knocking, and I was actually seeing stars. I did the network marketing verbal vomit, and the woman looked at me like a deer caught in the headlights!

I was so embarrassed that I went out to my car, called my mother (who's also my sponsor), and cried, "Do I go back in there?" "Nope, don't go back there," she replied. "Get out of there!" I cried the whole way home, wondering: *How will I ever be successful in network marketing if I can't even talk to people about my product?*

That was years ago. Since then, I've done hundreds—if not thousands—of successful presentations and have become one of the top presenters and prospectors in my company!

THE MULTIPLY METHOD

So, what changed?

I've gone through several iterations of presentations, and I've learned that the most effective ones are the ones that:

- Focus on the prospect
- Are short and sweet
- Don't require a script but are more conversational

Do you remember the meeting Rose had with Stacey, the prospect I was too chicken to chat with? Do you wonder what Rose said to get a highly successful entrepreneur to see the vision?

Do you recall the coffee get-together I had with Kathleen, the woman from the cookie shop? Are you curious about what I said to get her to join my business?

What both Rose and I said was powerful, professional, and, most importantly, highly duplicable—and you can have these types of conversations too!

Our presentation system is simple. When someone expresses interest in learning more, simply share: **WHY → WHAT → WHO**

Presenting is as simple as:

1. Sharing WHY you joined (your story)
2. Sharing WHAT you're doing (your company story)
3. Sharing WHO it is you're looking for (helping them connect their story)

PRESENTING: SHARING YOUR BUSINESS POWERFULLY AND PROFESSIONALLY

Then ask, "Who do you know that this would be great for?"

My presentation system has saved me time, helped me successfully recruit many people, and allowed me to create a simple yet successful presentation system for my team.

But let me first be vulnerable with you. I used to resent presentations—they were the one part of my business that I didn't love. In full transparency, they were huge time commitments—from the scheduling process to the time they took. I felt like I was constantly selling. Yet over time, I began fine-tuning my presentations so they would sound more like conversations. I also started shortening them, which made them more enjoyable for me *and* more effective for my prospects. Now, each of my presentations (or conversations) about the business usually lasts about fifteen minutes—perhaps a bit longer if anyone has additional questions.

Do you have a prospect who has agreed to hear more about your business? My tried-and-true, step-by-step presentation system can work over coffee, on a phone call, or even in a three-way presentation with one of your team members and your prospect. Here's how it works.

The First Step: Connect

The very first thing I do is connect with the individual. I start by saying: "Tell me, what excites you most about this opportunity? What would you like to learn more about today?"

THE MULTIPLY METHOD

I used to say, "Tell me all about you." Awkwardly, they would respond with, "Well, what do you want to know?" This would lead to uncomfortable silences, sometimes an hour of sharing life stories, and an awkward transition into talking more about the opportunity.

Now I've narrowed my presentation system to purposeful conversations with a simple question: "Tell me, what excites you most about the business, and what would you like to learn more about?" This allows me to focus on homing in on the prospect's interests and make sure I cater the conversation toward them—no script needed! If they talk about how exciting the product is, I dive deeper into that. If they talk about needing extra income, I know that's where my focus should be. I listen intently and take notes.

If it's a three-way presentation, I ask my business partner to fill me in on their guest before the call, so we aren't spending all our time getting to know one another. In this situation, the conversation might go something like this: "Thanks so much for your time today. Susie told me great things about you. She mentioned you're a Realtor and that you're great with people! We have so many Realtors who do really well in this business." Then I ask, "Tell me—what excites you most about the business? What would you like to learn more about?" I listen to their WHY, and then I share mine.

PRESENTING: SHARING YOUR BUSINESS POWERFULLY AND PROFESSIONALLY

The WHY

I thank them for sharing, and then I share why I joined the business and explain how it has allowed me to live more, give more, and do more. I might say something like, "Thanks so much for sharing. I'd love to share why I joined and what excited me most about this opportunity."

Share your truth about why you joined and what the business is allowing you to do.

"I was a teacher, and I was looking for a way to make extra income. When I found this business, I loved that it was low-cost and no-risk. I could do it on my time and on my terms, and I had the ability to become profitable right away. In part-time hours, the business allowed me to _____."

This last sentence is key. A lot of people have the misconception that they need a big-money story to make an impression, but that actually makes you *less* relatable. Instead, focus on what your business allows you to accomplish in part-time hours, such as:

- Funding your retirement
- Investing in new opportunities
- Contributing to your child's college fund
- Putting your kids in the school of your choice
- Paying off bills
- Giving to causes you're passionate about
- Contributing to the family income
- Traveling more

THE MULTIPLY METHOD

This approach helps you focus on meaning over money, and it's far more convincing than them judging your success by the size of your paycheck. Instead of evaluating your income, they're evaluating the impact the business has had on your life.

Essentially, you can say: "Here's why I joined [your reason], and what the business is doing for me or allowing me to do for others. In part-time hours, the business allows me to _____!"

Then you can transition with: "I'd love to share more about this business with you!"

The WHAT

Now it's time to talk more about what you're doing. This is the opportunity to share more about your product and the opportunity itself. As a social seller, you're selling two things:

1. A product
2. An opportunity

Here are some key topics to cover:

- **Partnership with the company:** What sets your company apart?
- **Products:** What results can people expect? What sets your products apart?

PRESENTING: SHARING YOUR BUSINESS POWERFULLY AND PROFESSIONALLY

- **Pay:** How do you get paid and recognized? What are some other perks?

- **Positioning and timing:** Why is now a great time to join?

Then share who it is you're looking for: "We're looking for people to try the products and get great results—and for people to join our fun and fast-growing team and profit by sharing their product results with others!"

The WHO

Now it's time to transition into WHO you're looking for and how one can enjoy the business. Ask: "Who do you know that the business or product would be great for?" Then add: "As we expand, we're looking for people who will try the products and get transformative results—and people who want to join us in business on our fun, fast-growing team."

There are two ways to be a part of this:

- **As a customer:** For example, you could share, "Our customer program gives you 10 percent off, free shipping, and a sixty-day guarantee—so you have nothing to lose, only great results to gain!" Then share your customer perks.

THE MULTIPLY METHOD

- **As a distributor of the product or a business partner:** Here, you can say something like, "As a distributor you get nearly 50 percent off your opening order, 25 percent off always, and the ability to use the products, get great results, and share a referral link with a friend. When you do, you can earn products for free, and you can even make some extra money when they join you!" Then share your distributor discount and tell more about the benefits of them joining you in the business.

Finally, I ask: "Who do you know that the business and products would be great for? Do you happen to have a personal interest in learning more?"

We will discuss the closing process in chapter 3, but my entire prospecting process, from conversation to close, looks like this: Prospecting > Presenting > Closing

Prospecting (Chapter 1) → Presenting (Chapter 2) → Closing (Chapter 3)

When you ask, "Who do you know?" they may identify others, just like Stacey did with Rose. This referral-based approach keeps the conversation positive, professional, and pressure-free, as you're simply "looking for people to join as you expand."

**PRESENTING: SHARING YOUR BUSINESS
POWERFULLY AND PROFESSIONALLY**

More Ways to Present

There are many more ways to present your business, some of which we'll cover in upcoming chapters. The goal is to teach your team the simple art of inviting and to have multiple ways for people to learn about your business. Here are a few:

Events

Events (live and virtual) are a powerful way to present both the products and the opportunity to large audiences. Hosting events, either in person, online, or a combination of both, is an effective way to invite people to learn about your business. I'll cover my step-by-step system for hosting events in the next chapter.

Recorded Presentations

If your company has recorded video presentations, share them with prospects so they can learn more about the business. You can also create your own videos. This way, all your team has to do is press play to share the presentation.

Three-Way Calls, Presentations, and Messenger Introductions

Using a third-party validation system (with your upline or teammate) is one of the most powerful tools for building belief and closing deals. Whether it's through a three-way call, a text, or a messaging app, involving a partner can help show prospects they're in good hands. Simply make introductions and have your upline ask: "What would you like to learn more about?" Listen and share—and use this chapter as a guide.

That's how simple presenting can be. And it works for anybody, in any company!

The Power of Presenting

When I first started in this business, I came across an article that had a profound impact on me. It helped me understand the real power behind presenting and why it's essential to keep pushing forward, no matter how many setbacks you face. I want to share the essence of that article with you because it might just inspire you to keep inviting and sharing your opportunity, as you never know who might say yes and change everything.

The article shared the story of a leader in our profession named Mark, who, at the time, was a minister in a small town in Texas. Mark was looking for change in his life, and he stumbled upon network marketing. Mark's sponsor gave him a bold promise: "This business can set you free financially in one to three years." But there was a catch. His sponsor also warned him of the challenges ahead, saying that in order to succeed, Mark would need to face and conquer three major "enemies" of the business.

PRESENTING: SHARING YOUR BUSINESS POWERFULLY AND PROFESSIONALLY

Enemy #1: Rejection

Mark was determined and ready for the challenge. He started by inviting two hundred friends to his house to watch a business presentation video. Unfortunately, eighty of them said no and declined his invitation.

Enemy #2: Deception

But Mark wasn't discouraged. He still had one hundred twenty people who showed up. Of those one hundred twenty, seventy watched the presentation. But guess what? Fifty-seven of them said, "Not interested."

Enemy #3: Attrition and Apathy

Determined to succeed, Mark pressed on. Thirteen people signed up. But, of course, not all of them stuck around. Twelve of those thirteen dropped out shortly afterward. Despite the setbacks, Mark didn't quit. He was left with just one person who was serious, but that one person ended up helping Mark earn over $50,000 per month—a result that changed his life.

Mark's story isn't unique. The article went on to tell the stories of many successful leaders in network marketing who have faced similar struggles—like Bill, one of the most successful distributors in our industry, who explained how he had shown his company's business plan to twelve hundred people. Out of those, nine hundred said no, and only three hundred signed up. Of those three hundred, only eighty-five did anything

THE MULTIPLY METHOD

with the business, and of those, thirty-five were serious enough to work on building the business. In the end, only eleven of those thirty-five truly made him a millionaire. After Bill worked through the numbers, he realized that success takes time, effort, and persistence.

I can relate to these stories in my own experience. In the beginning, I faced my own challenges, but I stayed committed. Over the years, I've done thousands of presentations and had countless conversations. I personally sponsored three hundred distributors in my first business. My organization grew to over three hundred *thousand* distributors, and our total team sales was over $2 billion per year—60 percent of which came from just six of the three hundred people I personally sponsored.

The lesson here is clear: Your success is directly tied to your willingness to work through the numbers and persist, even when things don't go as planned. Keep prospecting and keep presenting. Whether you are facing rejection, deception, apathy, or attrition, you must keep going. In fact, you might need to go through two hundred people to find the one individual who will become your star distributor. Are you willing to do that?

PRESENTING: SHARING YOUR BUSINESS POWERFULLY AND PROFESSIONALLY

I tell my team to track their nos, and I also tell them that hearing no is normal. I always teach my team that it's not *personal rejection*. It's simply *personal preference*. It is your job to share, and theirs to decide. But if you're willing to keep prospecting for potential leaders, and keep presenting, you will find those key leaders if you do not give up!

> YOUR SUCCESS IS DIRECTLY TIED TO YOUR WILLINGNESS TO WORK THROUGH THE NUMBERS AND PERSIST, EVEN WHEN THINGS DON'T GO AS PLANNED. KEEP PROSPECTING AND KEEP PRESENTING.

THE MULTIPLY METHOD

You see, there's no such thing as luck in this business. It's about being willing to keep talking to more people. If you're persistent, you will succeed. And as your skill level improves, your odds will improve too.

I've seen it firsthand, and I believe this is true for you too: *The numbers never lie.* If you talk to enough people and share your opportunity with enough prospects, you will find success.

> **IF YOU TALK TO ENOUGH PEOPLE AND SHARE YOUR OPPORTUNITY WITH ENOUGH PROSPECTS, YOU WILL FIND SUCCESS.**

PRESENTING: SHARING YOUR BUSINESS POWERFULLY AND PROFESSIONALLY

Application

Write Your "Short Story"

Here is WHY I joined: _____

_____

_____

_____

Here is WHAT the business is doing for me:
"In part-time hours, my business allows me to:

_____."

Map out your company story:

What makes your partnership with your company unique?
-
-
-

What sets your products apart?
-
-
-

Why are your pay plan, perks, and the model so powerful?
-
-
-

THE MULTIPLY METHOD

Regarding positioning and timing, why should others join you right now?

_____

_____

_____

_____

_____

Feeling more confident? Now let's CRUSH THE CLOSE!

CHAPTER 3

CLOSING: CONQUERING THE CLOSE AND COMMON OBJECTIONS

FRIEND, IF YOU'VE made it this far in the book—and you've started implementing the best practices for prospecting that you've learned about—chances are you've gotten people TO your prospecting funnel and THROUGH that prospecting funnel with a presentation. Now you're probably wondering how to get them INTO your business and off to a great start. That's what the next two chapters are all about—closing and enrolling!

I coach people in our profession for a living, and this is often the point where they get stuck. They feel confident generating leads, but they lack clarity on how to conquer the "close" and get prospects off the fence and into their business.

I can relate. It took me three months to close my first business partner. But since then, I've created a simple system for closing that not only helps you conquer the most common objections but also crush the close, bringing new people into your business with ease!

Simple Closing System

Before we dive into my simple system for closing, let's review the prospecting process:

Prospect → Present → Close

1. **Prospecting:** This is the art of inviting. To get people into my prospecting funnel, I start the process by giving them a compliment, engaging in conversation (by asking questions), and making a connection about my business, inviting them to learn more (as discussed in chapter 1).

2. **Presenting:** This is the system of sharing my business. Once a prospect agrees to learn more, I share the WHY (why I joined), WHAT (what the business is all about), and WHO (who we are looking for). I then ask, "Who do you know that this would be great for?" (as outlined in chapter 2).

3. **Closing:** Now that I have their attention, what do I do if they express interest? The *close* is all about taking the next steps to assess interest and asking for the order or enrollment.

CLOSING: CONQUERING THE CLOSE AND COMMON OBJECTIONS

Are you ready to crush the close?

Our Closing System (in Three Simple Steps)

Our closing system is simple and has three parts:

1. Identify Interest
2. Provide Information + Share Next Steps
3. Follow Up + Enroll

Identify Interest

In the previous chapter, we learned how to present your opportunity by sharing:

- **Why** you joined
- **What** the business is all about
- **Who** you're looking for
  (customers and business partners)

Then ask: "Who do you know that this would be great for?" Sometimes, they identify themselves.

Provide Information + Share Next Steps

When a person says they are interested in the product, I immediately say: "Great! I'd love to give you a quick consultation!" Then I guide them through my simple selling system, which we will review in the next chapter.

THE MULTIPLY METHOD

Selling System: Recommendation > Validation > Enroll

Recommendation
I ask: "If you could change one thing about your _____, what would it be and why?" (For example, "If you could change one thing about your skin, what would it be and why?") I then make a recommendation.

Validation
Next, I send before-and-after photos or testimonials about that product for validation. I might say something like, "My friends are loving it, and you're going to love it too!"

Create Urgency + Enroll
Create urgency and confidence by sharing any specials and your product guarantee. For example, you might say: "We have a _____ guarantee (or special), so you have nothing to lose. Would you like to give it a try?" Then, I enroll them as a customer: "I have a few minutes to get you started now—are you ready?"

When people express interest in the business,
Provide Follow-Up Info > Follow Up + Enroll
I say, "Here are the next steps . . . I'm going to send you a link to review the opportunity. I'd love for you to write down any questions you have. Let's set a time for a follow-up call where I can answer those questions.

CLOSING: CONQUERING THE CLOSE AND COMMON OBJECTIONS

And if you're interested in getting started, we can get you enrolled!" Then I send them the link to review, and we schedule the follow-up call.

The Follow-Up Call
This call is simple. I open the call by saying, "I'd love to hear what questions you have." This gives me the opportunity to answer questions and handle any objections (more on that shortly!).

After I've answered all their questions, I share what I call "Two Ways to Join." I'll explain, "Here are the two ways to start . . ." And then I give them more information:

- "Customers get these benefits . . ." (outline customer benefits and programs)
- "Distributors of the product get these added benefits . . ." (outline distributor benefits and programs)

Then I ask, "How would you like to start?"

Enroll
If they express interest in the product, I enroll them as a customer on the spot: "Here's what I recommend—would you like to give it a try?"

If they express interest in the business, I enroll them as a distributor: "Here's the best way to get started—are you ready to get started?"

THE MULTIPLY METHOD

Another Fun Way to Close

Here's another fun way to close, in addition to the Two Ways to Join approach, as I've outlined. At the end of your conversation or presentation about the business, ask: "On a scale from one to ten, how interested are you in joining us?"

- 1: They're ready to try the product and get results.
- 10: They're ready to join the business, get the best product discounts, and earn money by sharing their results plus a referral link with others.

What if they say they're anything less than a ten? Well, that just shows they have unanswered questions or objections. I then like to ask: "I'm curious—what would make you a ten?" This usually exposes any underlying objections they may have.

Overcoming Objections

First, I want to acknowledge that objections are totally normal. That's why I want to give you the tools and language to handle them confidently. When someone pushes back, it's not personal rejection—it's simply personal preference. And sometimes when someone says no, it doesn't always mean no forever. It could mean "not now" or "I don't know enough."

CLOSING: CONQUERING THE CLOSE AND COMMON OBJECTIONS

> **WHEN SOMEONE SAYS NO, IT DOESN'T ALWAYS MEAN NO FOREVER. IT COULD MEAN "NOT NOW" OR "I DON'T KNOW ENOUGH."**

That's why I like to validate their concern with what I call the Feel-Felt-Found method. It sounds like this: "I understand how you *feel* . . . I *felt* the same way when I started . . . but here's what I *found* out . . ."

Let's talk about how to overcome the most common objections using the Feel-Felt-Found method.

"No Money"
"I understand how you feel. I felt the same way when I started. Here's what I found out . . ." Write this down: *Facts tell, stories sell!* Anytime you can share a personal story, it helps people relate.

THE MULTIPLY METHOD

> **FACTS TELL, STORIES SELL! ANYTIME YOU CAN SHARE A PERSONAL STORY, IT HELPS PEOPLE RELATE.**

When I started my business, I was paying bills out of my family's savings. Things were tight. (Tell YOUR truth!) But I asked myself, *If nothing changes, what changes?* I saved up! Turns out, it was the best investment I ever made. Through our company's Fast Start program, I was able to earn back my return on investment within my first month. And now we have more money to save and invest.

Then, give them solutions to get started, explaining several ways people have saved up and gotten off to a successful start:

- **Saving:** Just like with any business, it's not uncommon to save to get started. Ideas to save up: sell household items online, sell clothes, or even pick up odd jobs. Let's brainstorm!

- **Preselling:** I've helped new distributors prelaunch their business by hosting an event, letting them borrow my products and preselling some items

CLOSING: CONQUERING THE CLOSE AND COMMON OBJECTIONS

that will come in their kit to the attendees, so they earn the money up front before they buy the kit.

Ask: "How can I help you get started?"

"No Time"

"I understand how you feel—many people felt the same way when they started, as we are all so busy! Here's what I found out: Most people start this business part-time alongside full-time jobs and very busy lives!"

Tell a story: "I remember when my business partner, Stacey, started—she had a forty-hour-per-week job, two young children, and a long work commute, but she was able to commit to working on the business an hour per day during her commute. She ended up building a successful business in under an hour each day, and she no longer has to trade hours for dollars. Now she has more time to spend with her family!"

Ask: "If I can teach you a way to do this successfully in under an hour per day, would that be of interest to you?"

Product Pricing

The key to this objection is to *build value*:

"I understand how you feel—I felt the same way too, but here's what I found . . ."

"We are a premium-priced product for premium results! The cost of our products is about [a cup of coffee per day]. When you add up what you'd pay at the store, it really isn't that different! The difference? The results people get!"

"We're so sure of the results, we offer a [sixty-day or whatever it is] guarantee!"

"Our [customer program] gives people the benefit of an additional discount. And if people still can't afford it, that's all the more reason to become a distributor. You can get our products at a great discount, earn them for free, or make some extra money as you get great results and share the products with others!"

Ask: "Would you like to learn more?"

"I Have to Think About It" or
"I Need to Ask My Significant Other"
"I understand completely! I'm going to send you some information to review, and let's schedule the follow-up call. The following times work best for me—when works for you?"

The goal is to give them the information to review and capture a time to quickly follow up.

"How Much Money Are *You* Making?"
I actually *love* this question—and you should too. Chances are, if you don't love it, you don't have a response ready that you feel confident with. Responding to this question with ease is key!

While I'm not a fan of sharing exactly how much I make, and I'm not sure why people feel so inclined to ask,

CLOSING: CONQUERING THE CLOSE AND COMMON OBJECTIONS

there's an effective way to answer it. When we respond with a dollar amount, not only does it feel "off," but it also gives them the chance to judge the validity of our opportunity. The truth is, success varies based on a variety of factors. Most people work the business part-time for a side income. So, instead of measuring success with money, I like to focus on *meaning*.

> **INSTEAD OF MEASURING SUCCESS WITH MONEY, I LIKE TO FOCUS ON MEANING.**

Write this down: "In part-time hours, my business allows me to _____." Then, fill in the blank:
- Send my kids to preschool
- Pay college tuition
- Invest
- Give generously to causes important to me
- Contribute to my family's income

THE MULTIPLY METHOD

Imagine when your prospect hears: "In part-time hours, my business allows me to pay for my kids' college expenses." WOW! That changes everything! You've attached money to meaning—and guess what? You unlock possibility for them too!
Ask: "What would your income goals be to get started?"

"I Don't Know Anyone!"
"I understand how you feel. I felt the same way when I started—I was shy with no network." (Tell YOUR truth!) "But here's what I found out . . ."
"The company has a simple system for social media that helps you generate more leads online. Can I teach you how it works?"
"The company has created a simple training system to help you grow your network and find new customers with ease."
Again, tell them more about company support and systems. Chances are, they just want to make sure they're going to be supported and successful.
Ask: "Can I tell you more about that?"

"I'm Not a Salesperson!"
I love this one because sometimes salespeople tend to struggle in our business. Our business is a relationship business that's not built on sales tactics. It's built on systems.
When I hear this objection, I often reply: "I

CLOSING: CONQUERING THE CLOSE AND COMMON OBJECTIONS

completely understand how you feel. I felt the same way. Here's my story!" I tell my story, and then say: "Our company provides simple systems to get customers and keep them happy for the long term!"

Ask: "Can I tell you more about my experience?"

"I Need to Try the Products First"

This is a common objection. If you're not prepared to handle it, your business could build at a snail's pace if everyone needs to "try it first." That's why it's important to lean on the credibility of your company, the effectiveness of your product, your personal results, and the company's guarantee.

"I understand how you feel. I felt the same way when I was getting started. But here's what I found out . . ."

"The company has great [before-and-after pictures] and [clinical studies] to provide social proof. Plus, you can lean into my story, the exciting testimonials we have, and the before-and-after examples the company provides as you build your own personal product story!"

Ask: "We have a company guarantee. Your best way to start in the business is by enrolling and leveraging the stories as you get your results and develop your own product story. Would you like to give it a try?"

"I Don't Want to Bug My Friends or Family"

I love when I get this one, too, because it comes from a place of caring. Truth be told, you're not bugging people unless you actually *are*. It's all about educating your prospects that there is a better way.

"I understand how you feel. I felt the same way when I got started. Here's what I found out. . .

"The company provides simple systems and scripts to help you expand your network beyond your existing connections. And for the people you *do* know, we teach you how to leverage a referral-based approach, so they feel like they're helping you, and you're not bugging them. Plus, when my friends start something new, I'm over the moon! I know your friends are going to be super excited for you too!"

Ask: "Can I share more about our approach?"

"No" (The Most Dreaded Objection Yet—or Is It?)

No is not a four-letter word—I promise! But these two letters can pack a big punch if you're not prepared for how to respond. The same is true for your team. That's why I like to prepare my new distributors with mindset training and equip them with the skill set they need when they hear this response.

I first let them know: "You are going to hear 'no' and that is normal. The business and products are not for everyone, of course!" Then I tell them that when someone says no, I want them to quickly respond with two words: "No problem!" And then I instruct them to say: "I'd love

CLOSING: CONQUERING THE CLOSE AND COMMON OBJECTIONS

to put you on my VIP list for exclusive offers and events!" (Then, put them on your list for follow-up!)

Sales 101: It takes an average of seven exposures before you hear a "Yes!"

This approach gives you permission to follow up.

When there's an event, I reach out to everyone on my VIP list: "Earlier you mentioned interest in the business. There's an exciting event happening this month that I'd love to invite you to as one of my VIPs! Would you like to be my guest?"

And when there's a special offer: "Earlier you expressed interest in the product. There's a sale I'd love to tell you about! My VIPs are the first to hear about it!" (Then share the special.) "If there's ever a good time to try, it's now!"

Ask: " Would you like to give it a try?"

The fortune is in the follow-up!

THE FORTUNE IS IN THE FOLLOW-UP!

Referral Rewards Program

Another thing to do when you hear no is to ask: "Who do you know that this would be great for? I build my business on referrals! I'd be happy to reward you for yours…"

THE MULTIPLY METHOD

Early on in my business, I developed my own referral rewards program. I was willing to invest product or a portion of my cash bonus as a finder's fee if someone referred me to someone who joined. It's an investment in your business that can have a huge ROI (return on investment)!

In the beginning of my career, my sister Emily told me no (her timing wasn't right). Even though I knew she'd be great for the business, I honored her no and said, "No problem. Who do you know that this would be great for? I would be happy to reward you for your referrals." I told her about my referral rewards program and let her know that if she referred people who joined, I would either give her free product or a portion of my cash bonus—her choice!

One day, Emily posted on social media about an upcoming event, as the company was expanding in her area. She mentioned that if anyone was interested, she would connect them with her sister (me!). A nurse saw the post and inquired about the event, and my sister connected her with me.

The nurse (who was also named Emily) came to the meeting and ended up joining us. I think I paid fifty dollars for that referral, and it turned out to be the best fifty dollars I ever spent! Emily the nurse went on to build one of the strongest sales organizations in our team. And my sister Emily *did* end up joining—ten years after telling me no. Her only regret? Not joining sooner and signing

CLOSING: CONQUERING THE CLOSE AND COMMON OBJECTIONS

up the other Emily herself!

As I told you, "no" isn't always forever—it may just be the timing isn't right. So keep in touch with people and always remember, the fortune is in the follow-up!

> "NO" ISN'T ALWAYS FOREVER— IT MAY JUST BE THE TIMING ISN'T RIGHT.

Application

Map out the Two Ways to Join method and practice your "close":

• Customer benefits:

• Business benefits:

Practice asking: "Which would you like to learn more about?"

What are some ideas you have for your own referral rewards program?

_____

_____

_____

_____

_____

CHAPTER 4

FAST START: STARTING NEW DISTRIBUTORS STRONG, EVERY SINGLE TIME

Now THAT YOU are bringing people into your prospecting funnel, through your funnel with presenting, and into your business by crushing the close, you're probably wondering, *Now that they're in my business, how do I get them off to a strong start?*

In this chapter, I am excited to share my simple system for starting people strong! When I am introduced onstage at company and industry events, often the person who's introducing me shares a fun fact: "Sarah has developed more personal leaders than almost anyone else in the profession!"

Remember earlier when I shared that most top leaders build their success with just a few successful legs or leaders? I have had fifty or more personally enrolled partners moving up the ranks in the business at any given time, and fifteen or more personally enrolled who have hit the very top ranks of the top of the pay plan. These are really good odds for our industry! I attribute this success—and the success of my team—to our Fast Start system.

Success starts in the very beginning with my Fast Start onboarding system for new distributors, which consists of:

1. Effective Enrolling
2. Goal Setting
3. List Building
4. Launching

Throughout this chapter, I am going to walk you step-by-step through the Fast Start system. This won't take the place of your company or team system, but it will enhance what you're doing and get you focused on the key areas where you should be spending most of your time.

Effective Enrolling

I believe good leadership starts at the enrollment appointment. When possible, I like to schedule time for this. During the enrollment, I go through the following:

- Enrollment Offers
- Website Walk-through
- Getting-Started Appointment

This enrollment appointment really serves as

FAST START: STARTING NEW DISTRIBUTORS STRONG, EVERY SINGLE TIME

on-the-job training, as we are in a business of duplication. Whatever they see you do in this appointment, they will duplicate in the business. This is why this appointment is so important!

Enrollment Offers
I believe in being a "product of the product," and a powerful way of sharing the product is having your own personal testimonial and, if applicable, before-and-after pictures.

Many times at enrollment, companies offer unique discounts to their distributors on their first purchase. It is my job not only to outline the value of the offer itself but also to note the value it will add to their business when they have a personal product testimonial to share. When we sit down for enrollment, I help my new partner make the product choice that best suits them, saying, "Here's what I recommend for you" and "Here's how most successful distributors start!"

Anytime they can get product at a discount at enrollment, it's a no-brainer! It allows them to:

- Become a distributor and be a product of the product —and get their first order at a really great price
- Have product to demo and display at events
- Have samples to share (when applicable)
- Receive product at the best savings, usually only at the time of enrollment

THE MULTIPLY METHOD

Next, if there are any other programs to enroll in that will give them more success, I tell them about these offers and help them effectively enroll, explaining the features and benefits. These can be things such as:

- Monthly orders/auto shipments
- Websites

And after they enroll, I make sure I congratulate them! Never forget how good it felt to start your first business!

Website Walk-through
This process involves walking your new business partner through any important company websites and team resources. These can include:

- Their website (I show them how to place an order and enroll a new team member.)
- Training resources or websites (I keep this brief so as not to overwhelm, but I empower them to find the information they need.)
- Community (I point out any places or pages where the team congregates or creates community.)

That enrollment call is almost like a first training call. It really is on-the-job training that gets them off to a great start! Toward the end of the appointment, we set

FAST START: STARTING NEW DISTRIBUTORS STRONG, EVERY SINGLE TIME

their first official training appointment—typically within their first twenty-four hours of joining—while their energy is high and they are excited!

The First Training

I like to set up a one-hour video call or in-person meeting to get them off to a great start! During this training, we cover:

- Setting goals
- Creating a list of people to invite to their launch
- Launching their business

Goal Setting

During this part of the process, I love to ask: "What is your WHY? And why are you doing this?" This is one of the most valuable conversations you will have as their sponsor. Then, dig deeper with questions like:

- What would a successful business look like for you?
- What would you do with the extra money?
- What would time freedom mean to you?
- How would you spend your time and with whom?

This allows me to help them make an emotional connection for when the times are tough. As we talked about earlier, there will be times you face rejection in business. And instead of being driven by doubts and disappointments, I want to help you stay focused on your dream.

THE MULTIPLY METHOD

Looking at the "big picture" is really effective for setting long-term goals. When you get your first "no," revisit your WHY. When your first customer or partner quits, revisit your WHY. This information will help you set goals.

> **WHEN YOU GET YOUR FIRST "NO," REVISIT YOUR WHY. WHEN YOUR FIRST CUSTOMER OR PARTNER QUITS, REVISIT YOUR WHY.**

Immediate Short-Term Goals
I then like to find out some immediate short-term goals by asking these questions: "What would a successful first month in business look like for you? How much would you like to earn?" Now, they may not know yet how to accurately answer that question, or even what is possible, so I might give some examples: "Is it to earn your return on investment?"

When you get the goal, give them a formula: "You can earn _____ when you _____."

Let's say the goal is to earn five hundred dollars. I

FAST START: STARTING NEW DISTRIBUTORS STRONG, EVERY SINGLE TIME

might say: "You can earn five hundred dollars when you enroll five new customers in the business!" Then I'll say: "How are we going to do that? Let's talk about that next!"

List Building

Your next steps are to help them "go for the goal" by:

- Creating their list of people with whom they want to share the business

- Hosting a launch event and teaching them how to invite people on their list to the event

Creating Their List

This is the next step of the getting-started training. The biggest question I get from new distributors is: "Who do I share this with, and how?" By helping them brainstorm *who* to invite and *how* to invite, you have the greatest chance of getting them off to a really successful start.

I tell them we are going to do a simple exercise of writing down names. I don't want them to pre-judge what people will say. We will talk about how to invite people in a bit, but first, let's just think about who they know, not what they are going to say. This is their chance to do a "brain dump." Who do they know on social media? Who is in their address book? Who do they interact with socially?

THE MULTIPLY METHOD

Memory Jogger

I like to start with a little memory jogger. Who do they know?

Family Members
- Mother/Father
- Grandmothers/Grandfathers
- Aunts/Uncles
- Daughters/Sons
- Granddaughters/Grandsons
- Mother-in-Law/Father-in-Law
- Nieces/Nephews
- Stepmothers/Stepfathers
- Stepdaughters/Stepsons
- Sisters/Brothers
- Cousins

Past Acquaintances
- Elementary School Friends
- Middle School Friends
- High School Friends
- College Friends
- Former Coworkers
- Hometown Friends
- Military Friends
- Former Teammates
- Summer Camp Friends

FAST START: STARTING NEW DISTRIBUTORS STRONG, EVERY SINGLE TIME

People You See on a Regular Basis
- Current Coworkers
- Church Members
- Current Friends
- Neighbors
- Supervisors
- Babysitters

Members of Organizations You Belong To
- Boys and Girls Clubs
- YMCA
- Rotary Club
- Fraternity/Sorority
- PTA
- Toastmasters
- Moose Lodge
- Elks Club

Those You Do Business With
- Lawyer
- Doctor
- Dentist
- Grocery Store Clerk
- Hairstylist
- Pediatrician
- Dry Cleaner Clerk
- Restaurant Server
- Car Salesperson

THE MULTIPLY METHOD

By giving them this list, it helps them think of who to invite to their launch event. I love to take list building to the next level by asking: "Who are your top ten dream team members?" and "Who, if your wildest dreams come true, would join you?"

This helps them to dream and envision these people on their team. Some people call this your "chicken" list because you may be too scared to reach out to these people first. I call it your dream team list because these are usually the people you should reach out to first!

When they identify the people on the list, I'll ask about each person: "Tell me more about them. Why did you choose them?" We then brainstorm together. I build their belief by validating them, getting excited with them, and sharing stories of people like them who are successful in the company.

For example, let's say their friend is a Realtor. I build their belief and create excitement by saying: "That person sounds great! Realtors do wonderfully in our business because they're great with people! Let me share with you the story of my friend Tracie, a Realtor who is very successful in our business." I love to share stories to build their belief that they should reach out to others. It also creates excitement for them to reach out to their friend and even gives them a story to share.

After we brainstorm ways to reach out and what to say, I give them the confidence to start inviting these people to their launch event. I also share a suggested

FAST START: STARTING NEW DISTRIBUTORS STRONG, EVERY SINGLE TIME

message of invitation, an email template to share with their list, and a sample post they can share on social media.

Launching

One of the most successful ways to start a new distributor is through a launch event.

My company is not a party-plan company, but I believe very strongly in launching a new distributor through a one-time event.

These events help them get their first customers to earn their first paycheck, and often make their first promotion in business. Events are also major belief builders! In fact, I can share countless stories of distributors who had thought about quitting—but since they had an event planned, they persevered, got their first taste of success, and are now some of the most successful distributors in their company today!

> ## EVENTS ARE MAJOR BELIEF BUILDERS!

Remember Emily the nurse? She was considering quitting, but because she had already scheduled her launch event and invitations had gone out, she decided to commit to hosting the event. At the launch party, people poured into the room to hear more about her product, and to her surprise, her friends were super supportive. She got several new customers and even connected with a few people who expressed interest in the business. Emily made her first promotion at the event, so she decided to continue. She eventually became one of the most successful sales leaders in the company!

This is why I love events for launching new people—they leverage a skill set people already know: *inviting*. Everyone's been invited to a birthday party before. It's a simple way to get new people started. You set them up to succeed. Most get their first crop of customers and earn their first check at a launch event. It's a simple way to start new people out strong!

Launch events can be in person, virtual, or even a live video—or a combo of all three! Either way, the goal is to get the news out to their network.

We will go more in depth on events in the next chapter, but for now, here's an overview of how I like to prepare a new business partner for their launch.

After we create the list of people to invite, the next question is: What will they invite the people on their list to? Their launch! Events are a key element to my onboarding system because it's so simple for the new distributor to simply set a date and focus on inviting.

The next step is to pull out our calendars to set the date for the event. The launch is like a grand opening to

FAST START: STARTING NEW DISTRIBUTORS STRONG, EVERY SINGLE TIME

their business. In fact, they can even call it that! When I initiate setting the date, I'll say to my new distributor: "Most successful leaders start with a launch event. Let's lock in the date! You focus on inviting. I'll do the heavy lifting for the event by helping you present and getting you all set up. And we will help you earn your first paycheck!"

Keep it simple for them so they aren't intimidated, and allow them to focus on inviting during their first few weeks in the business. So many people complicate the onboarding process with too many skills that they think their new partners have to learn right away. Instead, let them focus on inviting. That's simple!

Did you notice that I ease right into making the list and then say, "Now let's invite these friends to the launch of your business"?

I don't ask permission-based questions such as "Would you like to launch with an event?" I make a recommendation: "Here's how most successful leaders start! Let's set the date to launch your business with an event!" They enrolled with me because they trusted me with their success. The launch event is an important piece of their early success—and it's an important part of our systems.

When the world shut down in 2020, so did events, and this had a huge impact on our business. It made us realize how important events were to our onboarding process. Business slowed down when events had to stop.

THE MULTIPLY METHOD

Distributors weren't starting as strong. And it became clear that launching with an event is one of the strongest ways to get people started.

> **LAUNCHING WITH AN EVENT IS ONE OF THE STRONGEST WAYS TO GET PEOPLE STARTED.**

I try to schedule the launch event within the first few weeks of a new distributor's business. This is to get them going right away and keep their excitement high. It also helps them earn their first paycheck (and earn their return on investment) in the first month. Many will make their first promotions too.

If they are local, I help them host in person. If they are long distance, I help them present virtually. My main focus during their first few weeks of business is coaching them through inviting. When leaders make the mistake of overcomplicating their onboarding, it leads to overwhelm and a high turnover rate. My simple system (which is

FAST START: STARTING NEW DISTRIBUTORS STRONG, EVERY SINGLE TIME

largely focused on creating a list and inviting) is empowering and exciting. And getting started is simple:

1. Set goals. Then teach them how to achieve those goals by doing the following:
2. Creating a list of people to share with
3. Exciting those people + inviting them to an event

How and Who to Invite

After we've got the date on the calendar, it's time to focus on inviting. To make things simple for my new distributor, I provide the invitation language while they focus on personally inviting the people on their list to the "grand opening" of their business. They send out the invitations and share their excitement by making a personal call to amplify the invite: "There will be giveaways and a lot of fun!" "Your support would mean the world to me!"

When my mom and I started our business, we built a team of over three hundred distributors in our first month! People often ask what the key to our early success was. The answer is simple: events! We held an event every week and we would tell our team and guests, "We are doing this again next week—invite your friends!" And they did! We started many others successfully in the business by teaching them *who* to invite and *how* to invite.

THE MULTIPLY METHOD

> **WE STARTED MANY OTHERS SUCCESSFULLY IN THE BUSINESS BY TEACHING THEM *WHO* TO INVITE AND *HOW* TO INVITE.**

Let's launch!

FAST START: STARTING NEW DISTRIBUTORS STRONG, EVERY SINGLE TIME

Application

What are the key things you will incorporate as part of your Fast Start system for launching new partners strong?

_____

_____

_____

Based on what you learned in this chapter, what will you start doing, what will you stop doing, and what will you continue to do when launching a new partner in business?

- Start

_____

- Stop

_____

- Continue

_____

CHAPTER 5

EVENTS: LAUNCHING NEW DISTRIBUTORS STRONG

I'LL NEVER FORGET a phone call I once received from the CEO of our company at the time: "Sarah and Kris, you are going to have to slow down! We are growing so fast, we can hardly keep up with the growth!"

My mom and I had added three hundred people to our team in less than thirty days when we launched our business. The secret to our fast growth out of the gates? *Events!* During our first month in business, we held weekly events. Our organization is not a party-plan company, but we strongly believed that events were our fast track to success.

We held weekly gatherings at a coffee shop, where we would share both our opportunity and products and invite people to join us in the business. After giving a call to action and closing, we would tell people: "We are doing this again next week. Invite your friends!" And they did. We kept things so simple that all people had to do was *invite*!

Simple. Scalable. Successful. That's the power of events.

The Power of Inviting

Events are a fast track to growth, as you teach your team the simple skill of inviting. Think of it this way: Inviting is a skill that is second nature to most people. Almost all of us have invited someone to a party, for example. When you offer events, you make your business and systems so simple that all your distributors have to do is learn to *excite* and *invite*! Then they teach their teams to do the same.

> **WHEN YOU OFFER EVENTS, YOU MAKE YOUR BUSINESS AND SYSTEMS SO SIMPLE THAT ALL YOUR DISTRIBUTORS HAVE TO DO IS LEARN TO *EXCITE* AND *INVITE*!**

EVENTS: LAUNCHING NEW DISTRIBUTORS STRONG

As leaders, we had a polished presentation prepared; all our team had to do was invite others to it. This was the secret sauce of developing one of the fastest-growing teams in the industry.

When I run my coaching programs and masterminds with top leaders, I strongly express how important it is to hold events, especially when launching new distributors. Whether or not your company has a host incentive program, events are always one of the best ways to grow. That's because they're a great way to maximize your time and multiply your results.

> **EVENTS ARE ALWAYS ONE OF THE BEST WAYS TO GROW. THAT'S BECAUSE THEY'RE A GREAT WAY TO MAXIMIZE YOUR TIME AND MULTIPLY YOUR RESULTS.**

THE MULTIPLY METHOD

For new distributors, launching with an event is the fastest way to make their first promotion and earn their first paycheck. It's a simple way to get off to a fast start, as they are focused on just one thing: *inviting*. These events build belief and create a "stickiness" in the business. The new distributors are then excited for the next month, and they're continuing to learn as they earn.

I've heard countless stories of distributors on our team who said if it weren't for an event planned early in their career, they likely would have quit when doubt set in—but the invitations had already been sent out! After that first event, their belief was built as they saw how simple it was to share the products. They secured their first crop of customers and earned their first paycheck. In many cases, their rank advanced too!

Often people skip this simple step of activating with events and make the mistake of overcomplicating things for their new business partners. One of my business leaders, Emily, shared the story about how she had contemplated quitting, but because she already had invitations out for her launch event, she was willing to host it just this one time. To her surprise, at the event she got her first customers *and* a new business partner, made her first promotion in business, and earned her first paycheck. She went on to build one of the most successful teams in the company. What she'd thought would be a one-time event became part of her onboarding system for her team.

The only thing Emily had to focus on in her first

EVENTS: LAUNCHING NEW DISTRIBUTORS STRONG

month? Inviting others to her event! It was that simple. I coached her on the setup and cohosted the presentation with her. It built her confidence—and her early business success. This is why events are the best way to launch new distributors strong!

Let's talk about our simple system for in-person events:

- **Pre-Event:** Inviting
- **The Event:** Presenting
- **Post-Event:** Closing

Pre-Event: Inviting

Within their first two weeks, I like to set the event date to launch my new distributor. This is the event that will launch their business to their network.

Remember, the first things I do with new distributors are: Set goals, create their list, and then invite people on their list to their launch event. We go through our memory jogger list and invite everyone on it to their event. Of course, if the invitees are long-distance, the invitation is just an icebreaker to say: "I understand if you can't make it in person, but I'd love to share my new business with you!" Or they can stream the live event virtually and open it up to people who are out of town.

I create the invitation for my new distributor to keep feelings of being overwhelmed to a minimum and to empower them with a second-nature skill: focusing on

THE MULTIPLY METHOD

simply inviting. I also remind them that *the fortune is in the follow-up*! I recommend following up every invitation with a personal phone call. You can call or send a voice memo and say: "I want to be sure you got my invitation. I want to personally invite you to the grand opening of my business. Your opinion means the world to me, and it would mean so much to have you as my guest! Please join me for a night of networking and refreshments. I'll even be doing some fun giveaways and sharing free product samples. I can't wait to celebrate with you—can I count on you being there?"

Following up prior to the event (the night before) prevents last-minute cancellations. A simple reminder works well: "I'm so excited to see you tomorrow night. Confirming the [drink] menu—what is your preference? Thanks again for coming, it means so much to me!" This helps to ensure maximum attendance.

Another idea to increase attendance and maximize exposure is to allow your guests to invite a friend. I've even put entries into a drawing if guests are bringing a friend with them. When we cast a wider net, there is a greater chance that someone will want to try, buy, and learn more!

The first few weeks of a new distributor's business are solely focused on inviting and maximizing attendance at their event. Imagine that—you keep your distributor's Fast Start that simple. And they'll have great results at that event if they are focused on maximizing attendance. It's like on-the-job training. You earn as you learn, all while keeping the first month very simple.

EVENTS: LAUNCHING NEW DISTRIBUTORS STRONG

The Event: Presenting

I coach my new distributors mainly on the setup, so as not to overwhelm them. It is my responsibility as their sponsor to present and to help them host a successful event. If they are local, I go to the launch with them. If they are long-distance, I stream in virtually.

For the setup, I recommend the following:

1. **Have an ordering station.** Make sure you have physical copies or an electronic version of enrollment forms. Pens and catalogs are also great to have on hand.

2. **Display a product station and/or experience stations.** Have a place where the products are set up for people to see and try. If there is a way to experience the products, have a setup for that too. I also love having before-and-after pictures displayed next to each product. To build belief, share any places the products received press. You can put these in picture frames or laminate them and set them next to the products.

3. **Serve refreshments.** Keep it simple. Coffee and muffins. A basic charcuterie setup. Or if your company has shakes and snacks, serve those. This isn't meant to be a meal, but it can be used to keep people satisfied as you're closing the event, encouraging them to stay and mingle as you wrap things

up and take orders. Have your refreshments set up in a separate spot to enjoy after the presentation—this keeps people hanging out and talking a little longer!

4. **Use raffles to create excitement.** Raffles can be used to close more orders at the event and create a sense of urgency. Example: "Enter to win once you've placed an order, if you brought a guest, or if you agree to host an event."

5. **Take advantage of technology.** Show a video presentation or before-and-after examples when applicable. Be sure people can see and hear the presentation well, and test all the equipment prior to the event starting. If you are streaming virtually, you will want to test that too.

The Event Itself

I like to start events on time in order to be respectful of everyone's schedule and keep the event to under an hour. If you'd like to make time for networking at the beginning (and to signal an on-time start), you could add this information to the invitation:

6:30 p.m. — Networking
7:00–8:00 p.m. — Sarah's Launch!

EVENTS: LAUNCHING NEW DISTRIBUTORS STRONG

Here's a sample format of the launch event:
- Welcome/WHY
- Opportunity
- Product
- Call to Action/Close

Welcome/WHY

I like to have the new distributor/host welcome everyone to the event and share their WHY. This can be as simple as thanking everyone for coming, then sharing why they joined and what they are most excited about.

- Welcome
- Why they joined
- What the best part is

Here's an example of how to do this: "Thank you so much for coming! I'm so glad to have partnered with [XYZ company]. I was teaching kindergarten, looking for a way to supplement my income, when my friend introduced me to this opportunity. I loved that I could share these products, help more people, and supplement my income in part-time hours! I am so excited to share the products and more about the business with you today!"

THE MULTIPLY METHOD

Opportunity
I share my WHY and WHAT the business is doing for me and allowing me to do for others. Then, I share a little bit more about our opportunity. If anyone at the event is looking to work from home and make more money, I invite them to connect with us afterward on an exciting opportunity. Finally, I transition into the product: "What makes our opportunity so amazing are our award-winning products. Let me tell you more about them."

Product
Most people think they need a lengthy presentation on products, but that's where we can complicate things. The truth is, most of the products you present will not be for all of your guests. Instead of presenting each product individually, focus on a brief overview of the hero products (what differentiates them and sets them apart—features and benefits versus ingredients and details). Later, you can offer customized solutions for each guest during brief, one-on-one consultations after the presentation. Keep this part of the presentation at a high level.

Think of it this way: If a friend were to ask you to share more about your products, what would you tell them? Sell them on the idea of what problems your products solve and what makes them unique. If there are awards you've won, talk about them. If you have stories to tell, share them.

Give a brief overview of the products (including

EVENTS: LAUNCHING NEW DISTRIBUTORS STRONG

what they are and who they help) and, where applicable, share before-and-after images to build belief and provide social proof. Let guests know that each of them will get their own personal consultation where they'll learn about the product that's right for them. Encourage them not to leave before they get their fun, fast, and free consultation. (This is where you actually make a recommendation and secure a sale!) You can also share lots of validating stories and testimonials about the product.

The Close

Close your event by saying something like: "There are two ways to experience the products. As a customer, you'll get the following benefits _____." (Outline any benefits of your customer programs, creating desirability and urgency with any offers and guarantees.) Example:

"Our preferred customer program gives you 10 percent off and free shipping. And if you sign up tonight, we will waive your enrollment fee. All of our products come with a sixty-day guarantee, so you have nothing to lose!

"The second way you can join is by upgrading to the business opportunity for the following benefits _____." (Share the benefits of distributor discounts and so forth. Your goal is to create desirability for inquiring about the business.) Example:

"Many people prefer to enroll as a consultant. Consultants get 50 percent off at enrollment and 25 percent off always. Plus, they can earn free products and make extra money as they simply share their results with others. This option allows you to save more and to make money by sharing with others!" (Fill in the blanks with your company's offerings. The goal is to share both ways to join, emphasizing the benefits of becoming either a customer or a partner. I typically upsell to the business opportunity.)

Finally, direct them to the next steps: "In just a moment, I'll let you grab some refreshments and enjoy our product experience stations. We'll be going around and giving personal recommendations on the products. Hang tight until we get to you. You won't want to miss this!"

Then let guests mix and mingle while you focus on the close.

More About Personal Consultations + Closing the Event
As people mingle, meet for a personal consultation with each guest. Circulate the order forms and pull each person aside, asking this simple question: "If you could change one thing about your _____, what would it be?"

For example, if you sell skincare, ask: "If you could change one thing about your skin, what would it be?" Then respond to their answer with: "I have the perfect solution for you: _____." (Share the solution that addresses their problem and any specials.) Circle the item you recommend on the order form, then take them over to see the product and provide more details. This is where you actually sell the product!

EVENTS: LAUNCHING NEW DISTRIBUTORS STRONG

Ask: "Would you like to try it as a customer and get these benefits _____?" (Remind them of the customer benefits.) "Or would you prefer to join as a distributor and get these benefits _____?" (Remind them of distributor discounts and so on.)

Again, the goal is to introduce them to the business if they're interested. Circle what you recommend for them and let them know that if they fill out the form tonight and place an order, they will be entered to win the grand prize drawing. This creates urgency and excitement. If they're interested in the business, make sure to mark that on the form so you can follow up with them after the event.

Post-Event: Closing

You'll hear me say this a lot: *The fortune is in the follow-up!* When the event is over, be sure to call each guest and

1. Thank them for attending.

2. Ask if they have any questions about the products or the business.

3. Ask how they would like to get started—either as a customer or a business partner. Enroll them on the spot or set an enrollment appointment.

THE MULTIPLY METHOD

This is also a great time to say: "My business is expanding in your area. Would you be willing to host an event for me? You invite your friends, I'll do all the work, and I'll give you free product as a thank-you." This allows you to get in front of even more people!

Ongoing events are a great way to reach others. Imagine getting your product in front of many people in under an hour—and expanding into new networks as you share with your friends' friends!

> **IMAGINE GETTING YOUR PRODUCT IN FRONT OF MANY PEOPLE IN UNDER AN HOUR—AND EXPANDING INTO NEW NETWORKS AS YOU SHARE WITH YOUR FRIENDS' FRIENDS!**

EVENTS: LAUNCHING NEW DISTRIBUTORS STRONG

The Power of Events

When the world shut down in 2020, we definitely saw the effect events had on our business model. Half of our onboarding system was broken because we couldn't hold events to launch our new partners. We realized then just how powerful events were for the business. In fact, there is nothing like the impact of in-person events to build belief, create energy and excitement, and get maximum engagement. They allow people to experience your community and opportunity.

> THERE IS NOTHING LIKE THE IMPACT OF IN-PERSON EVENTS TO BUILD BELIEF, CREATE ENERGY AND EXCITEMENT, AND GET MAXIMUM ENGAGEMENT.

THE MULTIPLY METHOD

When in-person events are not possible or you're trying to engage more people as you expand into new markets, *virtual events* can be a great option. These can be done via an online meeting platform or live video.

Virtual Flow

Virtual events are another fun way to launch new partners and create ongoing opportunities for your team. I've hosted events with themes such as "Products + Possibilities," and I've even planned events for month-end closing calls for my team. I currently hold weekly virtual events for our team.

Just like our in-person events, my system for virtual events is broken down into three parts:

- **Pre-event**
- **The event**
- **Post-event**

Pre-Event
I recommend that you don't just drop people into presentations. Personal invitations are key to getting attendance and providing a personal touch. Similar to in-person events, you'll want to personally invite people to virtual events, giving them instructions for joining and telling them how much the event means to you and how excited you are for them to attend.

EVENTS: LAUNCHING NEW DISTRIBUTORS STRONG

Here's an example: "I'm reaching out to our VIPs! Earlier, you expressed interest in _____. We're hosting an awesome night of networking, giveaways, and sharing great information on the business. Would you be my personal guest?"

Don't forget to extend a same-day reminder—perhaps an hour before the event is scheduled to begin—and send another reminder as the event is starting to ensure everyone was able to get on OK.

Because it's hard to create accountability for virtual events, it's important to message the people on your guest list as the event starts: "Just wanted to be sure you made it on OK!"

The Event
Welcome + Share WHY
Welcome guests to the event and share your short story:

- **Welcome**
- **Why you joined**

Ask guests to share in the chat:

- **Their WHY**
- **What the business is doing for them or allowing them to do for others.**

This process builds belief and provides social proof for the guests. It also creates great engagement in the chat. You can read some of these out loud as testimonials as you open your presentation. Prep your team ahead of time to respond when you ask. Also, invite guests to say hi and mention who invited them.

Share the Opportunity

Similar to the live event, in a virtual meeting you can share more about the company and the opportunity using these bullet points as a guide:

- **Partnership with the Company:** Tell more about your business and what sets it apart. Then transition into the products: "What makes our opportunity so incredible are our award-winning products."

- **Products:** Give a high-level overview of the products. What results can people expect? What makes them unlike anything else on the market? This is a good time to share stories or before-and-after images, as outlined in the following.

- **Plan and Pay, and How to Participate:** Share the two ways to try the product: as a customer (explain their benefits), or as a partner (explain their benefits).

- **Positioning and Timing:** Why is now a great time to join? Share any offers on enrollment (customer or partner) and any guarantees.

EVENTS: LAUNCHING NEW DISTRIBUTORS STRONG

When You Share the Products

Because virtual events don't have an opportunity for live interaction with products, it's imperative to showcase them with product results. You can do this by sharing product testimonials and before-and-after photos on the screen. Also, hold up the products as you're talking about them.

Similar to the live event, give an overview of the products:

- The philosophy behind them
- What sets them apart
- What makes them unique

Focus on the features and benefits, showing before-and-after photos as you talk, and asking for guest testimonials in the chat. To make the event interactive and build excitement, read those testimonials aloud.

The Close

Let people know there are two ways they can try the products:

- **As a customer:** Share any specials—and anything else that's applicable—about your customer program.

- **As a distributor:** Share any enrollment specials and explain more about the savings and benefits of being a distributor.

Let them know that their friend who invited them will follow up to share information about how to join, give personal recommendations, and answer all their questions.

Remind your team: *The fortune is in the follow-up!* This cues your team to follow up.

Post-Event

I coach my team to reach out to their guests after events and do the following:

1. Thank them for attending.
2. Ask them what questions they still have.
3. Ask them how they would like to get started—either as a customer or a business partner. (Then, they can enroll them on the spot or set an enrollment appointment.)

This is also a great time to mention this: "My business is expanding in your area. Would you be willing to host an event for me?"

Virtual events are a great way to expand into new markets!

> **VIRTUAL EVENTS ARE A GREAT WAY TO EXPAND INTO NEW MARKETS!**

EVENTS: LAUNCHING NEW DISTRIBUTORS STRONG

More on Events

I've hosted countless events over the past two decades, and they remain one of the best ways to create excitement and engagement about the products and the company.

Fun Event Themes
- Cocktails and Conversation
- Coffee and Conversation
- Spooky Spa Party
- Products and Possibilities
- Lunch and Learn
- Customer Appreciation
- Giving and Gratitude
- New Year, New YOU!
- Birthday Bash
- Sip and Shop
- Sip and Share
- Mingle and Jingle
- Profession-based events (e.g., teachers, nurses)
- Back-to-School Bash
- Pampering Party
- Opportunity Pop-Up (Opp Pop)
- Opportunity Open House
- Wellness Workshop
- Charity-themed events (e.g., donate a portion of the proceeds or guests donate toys)
- Summer Soirée

THE MULTIPLY METHOD

- "Fall" in Love with Your _____
- Galentine's Day (Fondue + Facials)
- Month-End Closing Call
- Virtual Beauty Bash
- Leave the Aging to Wine + Cheese

Other Types of Events to Consider

Trade Shows

Trade shows are a great way to get your business in front of more new people.

- **Why I love them:** You're surrounded by other smart, entrepreneurial businesspeople who are also promoting their products. I've found amazing leaders for my business in this way.

- **How to find them:** Local chambers of commerce, networking groups, local schools and churches, Google searches for vendor events in your area.

- **How to set up:** Push your table to the back of your booth to create an open space for people to walk around in. Display your products and have a giveaway front and center to attract people. Don't forget raffle forms (this helps create a "leads list") and order forms too.

- **Tips for getting customers:** Invite people to enter to win your free raffle! Have them fill out a form (this gives you their contact info for follow-up). As they're filling it out, ask them: "If you could change one thing about your _____ what would it be?" Then, show them what you recommend, talk to them about the product, and tell them about any offers you have. You may make a few sales this way, but remember: *The fortune is in the follow-up!* Since you'll only have one raffle winner, you can connect with everyone else who entered with a "gift with purchase" offer if they order after the event.

- **Tips for getting business partners:** As I mentioned, I've found great leaders at trade shows, and most of them were also hosting booths. I like to arrive early and set up, giving myself time to connect with other vendors and show interest in their products. I'm also usually the last to tear down so I can spend the end of the event going back around to everyone's booth, sharing a sample of my product, and getting contact information so I can stay in touch and follow up.

Conclusion

It's amazing how much impact events have. They are a fantastic way to get new business partners and more customers. And speaking of customers, it's time to talk about my customer acquisition system that has created a million happy customers and billions in sales per year! Are you ready?

> IT'S AMAZING HOW MUCH IMPACT EVENTS HAVE. THEY ARE A FANTASTIC WAY TO GET NEW BUSINESS PARTNERS AND MORE CUSTOMERS.

EVENTS: LAUNCHING NEW DISTRIBUTORS STRONG

Application

Schedule an event for this month or next. Who will you invite?

_____

_____

_____

_____

_____

_____

_____

_____

CHAPTER 6

CUSTOMER ACQUISITION AND RETENTION: HOW TO GET CUSTOMERS AND KEEP THEM

We've built a billion-dollar sales team—which is made up of hundreds of thousands of distributors who serve millions of customers. To build long-term, sustainable success in our business, the ultimate goal is to create an army of customers and keep them happy.

The key to acquiring customers is through a simple selling system, and the key to retaining them is through a strong customer retention system, complete with follow-up. Once you have an army of happy customers using your product, you want to keep them because they are your best brand ambassadors. In fact, the majority of our partners started first as customers.

Think of it this way: Your wildest dream come true is having an army of happy customers who upgrade to become your brand ambassadors. They already love the product—why not let them enjoy a great discount, earn free products, and even make a little extra money by simply sharing their story with others?

I got my start as a customer and then as a distributor. I had bad adult acne and had tried everything, but nothing seemed to be working to clear my skin. I was introduced to our product by my mother, and immediately after I started using it, my skin's redness went down and the swelling decreased—and today I am acne-free! Because of my positive results with the product, I was able to share my story with excitement, creating a great base of customers simply by sharing my personal testimony and before-and-after photos.

> **TO BUILD LONG-TERM, SUSTAINABLE SUCCESS IN OUR BUSINESS, THE ULTIMATE GOAL IS TO CREATE AN ARMY OF CUSTOMERS AND KEEP THEM HAPPY.**

CUSTOMER ACQUISITION AND RETENTION: HOW TO GET CUSTOMERS AND KEEP THEM

When I started my business, I worked very part-time, as I also had my full-time teaching job. Initially, I shared the product with everyone I knew. I was able to earn a few hundred dollars per month, which eventually grew to a few thousand dollars per month. All of this was residual income as my customers kept reordering. I eventually replaced my teaching income that first year. This was great "part-time" income with product sales.

One of the best things you can do for your new team members (and yourself) is to build their confidence (and paychecks) by helping them acquire their first set of customers, whether that's through a launch event or other strategies shared in this chapter. When you have an army of happy customers ordering your product, it's your wildest dream come true. And remember, you can always talk to them about upgrading to the business later.

Customer Acquisition System

To sell a product, you must first be a product of the product! And to attract customers, it helps to have a personal experience with the product, along with your own product story (a.k.a. your testimonial). You can share your product story in a variety of ways, including:

- Before-and-after pictures
- Testimonials (your story and the stories of others)

THE MULTIPLY METHOD

Before-and-After Photos/Progress Photos
Success in selling is all about storytelling, not "selling." So, how do you tell a story?

> ## SUCCESS IN SELLING IS ALL ABOUT STORY-TELLING, NOT "SELLING."

One of the best ways to tell a story is by showing proof that the products work—through before-and-after photos or progress pictures. If you have a product that shows physical results, you must be a product of the product. So, track your results and share them!

I have a digital album where our team contributes before-and-after pictures of themselves and their customers who have given us permission to share their results. I also keep an album on my phone of before-and-after examples. This way, when I'm talking about a product, I have a before-and-after image I can pull up. This is one of the greatest ways to provide social proof: *Show, don't tell!* Show people the results.

I encourage my team members to start using the product, take a before picture, and ask everyone in their circle to do the same. I tell them that tracking their results with a photo every thirty days (or as recommended by

CUSTOMER ACQUISITION AND RETENTION: HOW TO GET CUSTOMERS AND KEEP THEM

your company) and sharing those results with others is the easiest way to "sell" the product. If you don't have a product that provides physical results, there are other effective ways to sell your product. One of them is *testimonials*.

Testimonials

If you don't have progress photos or before-and-after images to share, another great way to provide social proof is through testimonials. Want to know how to get a testimonial you can use? Text your best customer and ask, "How are you loving your product?" When you get a response, ask if they'd be OK with you sharing it. Tag them on social media. Share it in your text or email marketing.

I've seen network marketers and marketers sell everything from low-cost items to high-ticket offers through testimonials. Generate as many testimonials as you can. Create a library full of them—and be sure to sprinkle them into anything you use to promote your products, including events, newsletters, or social media. Social proof leads to more sales.

Your own testimonial is another powerful way to sell your product.

Sharing Your Product Story

Facts tell, stories sell! There is no greater way to share your product than through your personal testimonial. I like to create a story outline for my team that helps them package their story in a professional way, in under a minute. Here's a sample outline you can use:

1. What was your problem prior to finding the product or service?
2. What product or service did you use to solve your problem?
3. What initial results did you see?
4. What is the best part of using the product?

> **FACTS TELL, STORIES SELL! THERE IS NO GREATER WAY TO SHARE YOUR PRODUCT THAN THROUGH YOUR PERSONAL TESTIMONIAL.**

My story might sound something like this: "I was struggling with adult acne. I searched for years for a solution, but nothing I tried worked. Then I found our acne line and decided to give it a try. I was amazed! Instantly, the redness went down and my swelling went down too.

CUSTOMER ACQUISITION AND RETENTION: HOW TO GET CUSTOMERS AND KEEP THEM

And the best part is, today I am acne-free and have the best skin of my life!"

People generally don't want to hear all about the ingredients and details—they just want to know one thing: "Does it work?"

Can you see how a short, punchy story can create powerful proof when talking about your product? We often make a big mistake in thinking we need to explain all the ingredients and details, when the customer really just wants to know: "Will this work for me?"

Stories are such a great way to sell a product!

Great Ways to Acquire Customers

- Events
- Social Media
- Referrals
- Sampling

We touched on referrals and events in previous chapters, and we will discuss social media best practices in the next chapter. Now let's talk about how to leverage "smart sampling" to get new customers through our sampling system.

Sampling
When it comes to sampling, I believe in being smart. I always tell my team: "A sample without a name is money

down the drain." And (of course!): "The fortune is in the follow-up!"

I'm all about running a profitable business, and using samples incorrectly can lead to wasted money and wasted time. But when done correctly—with follow-up—sampling can be very beneficial. As with anything in our business, *the fortune is in the follow-up!* Let's talk about how to make a sampling system work for you.

> # A SAMPLE WITHOUT A NAME IS MONEY DOWN THE DRAIN.

First: What Not to Do
Don't freely hand out samples, thinking they're going to lead to getting more customers. How many samples have you thrown in a drawer and forgotten about? You want to use samples strategically; otherwise, you're wasting your money and your time, and there's a good chance that those samples you randomly give out may end up in someone else's "product graveyard" drawer.

When you use sampling as a strategy, consider leveraging it as a conversation starter—and make sure there is follow-up attached.

CUSTOMER ACQUISITION AND RETENTION: HOW TO GET CUSTOMERS AND KEEP THEM

Example: Conversation Starter with Samples

Let's say you see someone you'd like to talk to about your business. First, remember our system:

Compliment → Conversation → Connection (Sample and Social)

Here's how it works.

Let's say someone gives you great service. You *compliment* them: "Thanks for your great service today! How long have you worked here?"

Then, you continue the *conversation* by asking questions: "Do you love what you do?" "Is this full-time or part-time work for you?" Make sure you show genuine interest in the other person!

At the end of your conversation, you *connect* and say: "I've loved chatting with you today—and I'd love to leave you with a little gift. If you promise me you'll use it, I promise I'll follow up and stay in touch. Are you on social?"

Tell them more about the sample. Connect on social media. Set the follow-up appointment. Then *actually* follow up!

Another Example

You meet someone when you're out running errands or at a kid's game. You *compliment* them: "I love that bag! Can I ask, where did you get it?"

You continue the *conversation* by asking questions. Be genuinely interested in them.

At the end of your conversation, you *connect* and say: "I've loved chatting with you today—and I'd love to leave you with a little gift. If you promise me you'll use it, I promise I'll follow up and stay in touch. Are you on social?"

Tell them more about the sample. Connect on social media. Set the follow-up appointment. And then *actually* follow up!

The biggest mistake I see people make is *not following up* after gifting a sample. Remember: *A sample without a name is money down the drain! The fortune is in the follow-up!*

Follow-Up System for Sampling

So, what do you do after you've given someone a sample? Follow up! Simple as that.

Always ask when would be a good time to follow up, and confirm. Then set a reminder and stick to it. What do you say when you follow up? Here's our simple follow-up system for sampling:

1. Share how nice it was to meet them.

2. Ask how they liked the sample and what questions they have.

3. Offer them a personalized consultation for the product.

CUSTOMER ACQUISITION AND RETENTION: HOW TO GET CUSTOMERS AND KEEP THEM

Here's how that may sound: "Hi Sue, it's Sarah. How are you? It was so awesome meeting you on Saturday!" (Pay a genuine compliment or recall a part of your conversation. Catch up for a bit.) "I'd love to know what you thought of the sample." (Have a conversation about the product they tried.) "Can I offer you a personal consultation? Do you have a minute to learn more about what we offer? It's fast, fun, and free."

- Ask: "If you could change one thing about your _____, what would it be and why?"

- Make a recommendation and send accompanying before-and-after images or testimonials to provide product validation.

    Share how much they would love it, and how much your customers love it.

- Share any specials or guarantees on the recommended product.

- Ask: "Would you like to give it a try?" Remind them of any offers or guarantees.

This can lead to an order or interest in the product.

Samples should always be used strategically either to start a conversation or secure an order.

Securing an Order with Samples

I don't believe in using samples in the traditional sense of trialing a product—this can actually delay the sales process and cost you a lot of time and money. Instead, I use samples to start a conversation about the products (as described previously) *or* to secure an order.

A good example of this is a gift with purchase—just like in department stores. Have you ever noticed that the salespeople at cosmetics counters usually slide samples into your bag with your purchase? That is strategic. It's to introduce you to something that may complement your order in the hope that next time, you'll buy even more products.

Use your own samples strategically—and always remember, the fortune is in the follow-up!

Now that you know where to find people to buy with "words that work," let's talk about securing a sale with a simple selling system.

My Simple Selling System (Customer Acquisition)

Once someone expresses interest in my product, I go through the following steps of my customer acquisition system:

Recommendation→ Validation→ Enrollment

I first start with a recommendation, then I provide validation that the products work, and lastly I lead them to an enrollment.

CUSTOMER ACQUISITION AND RETENTION: HOW TO GET CUSTOMERS AND KEEP THEM

> I FIRST START WITH A RECOMMENDATION, THEN I PROVIDE VALIDATION THAT THE PRODUCTS WORK, AND LASTLY I LEAD THEM TO AN ENROLLMENT.

Recommendation

Any time someone inquires about my product, I say: "I'd love to make a recommendation for you. If you could change one thing about your [skin, health, makeup routine—whatever it is you sell] what would it be and why?"

If your company has a tool to provide a recommendation, use that to help you. Then make your recommendation: "Based on your feedback, I recommend _____ for you."

Validation

This is where people make the mistake of "selling" or giving too much information, which can lead to overwhelm. Instead, send the recommendation with a few testimonials or before-and-after pictures that go along with the product you recommend.

You can say: "You're going to love this product! Our customers love it too. Check out these results!" Then, share before-and-after images or testimonials.

Enrollment

Create urgency by going right into sharing an offer or your company guarantee: "We have a sixty-day, empty-bottle guarantee, so there's nothing to lose. Plus I can offer you free shipping today. Would you like to give it a try?"

Always ask: "Would you like to give it a try?" You have not if you ask not!

If someone says yes, I immediately offer an enrollment appointment: "Let's get you started now! It takes just a minute." Then I take the order right there on the spot.

This, my friends, is our simple selling system:

Recommendation → Validation → Enroll
(ask for the order)

You have not if you ask not. So get your ask in gear! And now that you have some customers, let's talk about how to keep them!

CUSTOMER ACQUISITION AND RETENTION: HOW TO GET CUSTOMERS AND KEEP THEM

Customer Retention System (Five Questions to Ask in Your Follow-Up)

Treat your customers like royalty, and they will give you loyalty! This has been my mantra since I started my business. It's no wonder our team has served millions of customers and done billions of dollars in sales! It's why a majority of our customers upgrade to being business partners and create their own sales teams. This is how our business has MULTIPLIED!

> **TREAT YOUR CUSTOMERS LIKE ROYALTY, AND THEY WILL GIVE YOU LOYALTY!**

Just as important as getting a customer is keeping that customer for the long term. This is how you create a steady stream of residual orders. Your wildest dream come true is an army full of happy customers who are always ordering your product. That's why I always say: "Customer service is king!"

I'll give you a good example of my own customer service experience. I have a customer service person I've shopped with for years whose name is Travis. He always goes above and beyond when it comes to customer service.

THE MULTIPLY METHOD

Therefore, my connection with him never feels transactional but relational.

Travis will text me just to see how our family is doing or wish me a happy Mother's Day or birthday. One day I even showed up to a team retreat and saw he had sent flowers to wish us a great time. The result? I go out of my way to give Travis my business. Not just to shop with him, but also to refer other people to him. When Travis reaches out to share a special or something he thinks I would love, I appreciate it. He's earned my business by going out of his way to build a relationship with me. And I trust him.

Now let me tell you about a text I received from a woman at a different department store—someone who only texts me when there's something she wants me to buy. I look at it totally differently because our relationship is transactional, which actually isn't a relationship. To be honest, I usually don't respond to her. Nobody wants to be "sold to," but people are compelled to do business with you when you prioritize a relationship with them.

Travis has earned the right to message me with something he thinks I would love because he's focused on relationship over revenue—people over profit—and at the end of the day, he's a person with whom I love doing business.

What about you? Are your interactions with your customers transactional or relational? Are you prioritizing people over profit—and relationship over revenue?

CUSTOMER ACQUISITION AND RETENTION: HOW TO GET CUSTOMERS AND KEEP THEM

Think about a time when you received great (long-term) customer service—and a time when you felt the relationship was only transactional.

Now think about your own customers. Do you know their birthdays or anniversaries? Do you know who and what is important to them? Do you reach out to them to offer great service? Do you sometimes reach out to them "just because"?

Remember, we are in a *relationship* business. People prefer to do business with those they know, like, and trust—and at the end of the day, those are the people who get referrals too.

> WE ARE IN A *RELATIONSHIP* BUSINESS. PEOPLE PREFER TO DO BUSINESS WITH THOSE THEY KNOW, LIKE, AND TRUST.

Once you get a great customer, it's so important that you stay in touch and keep them happy for the long term. That's why my customer retention system involves

THE MULTIPLY METHOD

five simple questions that I ask monthly to ensure I stay in contact with my customers and keep them content. This system is the key to getting regular orders, reorders, and referrals—even upsells and upgrades into the business. My customer retention system has the power to change your business and build long-term, sustainable sales and success.

Are you ready for it?

Customer Retention System in Five Simple Questions
Every month, I reach out to my customers, asking them a series of five questions. But before I ask them anything, I touch base, thank them for being my customer, and do a little catch-up. I ask them what's new and exciting in their life, and then I check to see how they're doing with their products.

I then ask them the following five questions (which you can modify based on your own product offerings):

1. How are you loving your product?
2. What are you low on that I can help you replenish this month?
3. Can I share something new (or an exciting offer) with you?
4. As a distributor, I get great benefits—are you interested in learning more about that?
5. I build my business on referrals—do you know anyone who this product or business would be great for?

CUSTOMER ACQUISITION AND RETENTION: HOW TO GET CUSTOMERS AND KEEP THEM

Let's dig a little deeper here. The reason I ask, "How are you *loving* your product?" is that a positive question usually elicits a positive response. This is also a great time to troubleshoot with your customers and help them get the best benefits. Spend a little bit of time getting their feedback.

I then ask what they are low on that I can help them replenish. If you have a consumable product, you will want to ask this, too, as this is key to getting regular orders—every month versus every now and again. Think of it this way: When you run out of something, you are far more apt to order another item at the most convenient place at the time you need it. So if you want regular orders, this is key to staying top of mind. Fulfill before they forget and order something else out of urgency or necessity. This is key to regular orders and reorders.

Next, share something new with them. This is the key to upselling and increasing your average order value. It's like fast-food restaurants asking, "Do you want fries with that?" The goal is to increase the average order of each customer and uplevel their results. This is the perfect time to recommend something new that you think they would love—a new product, a special, a sale the company is having, or something that would complement the current products they are using. This is the key to upsells.

This next tip is the ultimate—the key to upgrades! Remember when I mentioned that the majority of our business partners started first as customers? This is an

THE MULTIPLY METHOD

essential part of my customer acquisition system—introducing the business. Customers make the best business partners! I will usually say: "I'm not sure if I mentioned this recently, but being a distributor of the product gives me great benefits. Would you be interested in learning more?" I share what those benefits are—discounts, perks, free products, extra income. A simple ask—"Would you like to learn more?"—can open up a conversation about the business. And remember, your customers make your best brand ambassadors! This is key to upgrading to the business. Would you rather have one sale from the customer—or multiple points of sale when that customer becomes a partner and starts sharing their results with others and making additional sales?

Finally, remember to thank them and ask for referrals: "Who do you know that the business and product would be great for?" If you have a referral rewards program, as we mentioned in an earlier chapter, this would be a great time to introduce them to it.

This simple system has been key for customer retention: regular orders, reorders, referrals, upsells, and upgrades into the business. Try it out—you'll be amazed at the results!

Are you ready to crush your customer sales? Let's go!

And do you want to know how I start so many of those conversations? In the next chapter, I'll share how to sell more plus sponsor more on social media.

**CUSTOMER ACQUISITION AND RETENTION:
HOW TO GET CUSTOMERS AND KEEP THEM**

Application

It's time to call your customers! Using our five points of follow-up, start reaching out:

Customer Name	Contact Info	Follow-Up Notes

THE MULTIPLY METHOD

Follow-Up: Five Questions to Ask When You Touch Base

1. How are you loving your product?

2. What are you low on that I can help you replenish this month?

3. Can I share something new [or an exciting offer] with you?

4. As a distributor, I get great benefits—are you interested in learning more about that?

5. I build my business on referrals—do you know anyone who the product or business would be great for?

CHAPTER 7

SOCIAL MEDIA THAT SELLS: MY SOCIAL MEDIA SELLING SYSTEM

ALL RIGHT, FRIEND, this is where things get fun! I'm so excited for the strategy that I'm about to share. In fact, it's how I generate the majority of my leads . . . and how most of them come to me!

This is what I'm known for in my coaching program, the Network Marketing Inner Circle—next-level lead generation on social media. We don't just coach you—we help you generate leads alongside you! It's so cool to see people generate leads online in real time. And we celebrate the wins of our students every single week. I love this stuff!

We are in a social selling business, and for that reason, I love to share my business on social media. I am the number one recruiter in my company, and the majority of my leads come to me online. Generating leads on social is my superpower in business! In fact, it's why most people join my coaching programs. It's such a successful strategy that when I teach my students to track their insights and results, they are amazed by their growth on social media. They're able to grow both their number of followers (who are potential customers) and engaged followers (who love their great content). My coaching clients and I generate leads together in real time, online. And because social media is changing all the time, we stay up-to-date with all the latest strategies.

Since social media is constantly changing, we won't go into the specifics of certain platforms, but we *will* talk about what works and what doesn't work when it comes to "selling on social."

If you need specific strategies and want to stay up-to-date with "what's working now" on social media—and how to prospect on all the latest platforms—I recommend you join us in our Network Marketing Inner Circle coaching group, as we keep our students up-to-date on the latest social media strategy and systems.

For now, let's discuss a selling system on social media that will help you generate new leads online, increase your followers, and boost engagement. More followers means more potential customers for you!

Having Success on Social Media

Before we talk about what's working, you need to know what's *not* working when it comes to having success on social media. So many social sellers get it wrong. They

SOCIAL MEDIA THAT SELLS:
MY SOCIAL MEDIA SELLING SYSTEM

go in with the mindset that social media is a task they have to check off their list. They simply go online, post their product, and wonder why they aren't getting new leads. In fact, their efforts often have the opposite effect of what they hope for: They lose followers, and sales slow down.

Write this down: *Your business is your priority, not theirs!* And this: *Your product is only one solution to the many problems your prospect faces.*

> # YOUR PRODUCT IS ONLY ONE SOLUTION TO THE MANY PROBLEMS YOUR PROSPECT FACES.

Boom! That's a mic-drop moment.

In other words, your selling on social is not exciting to your audience. Truth be told, if you're doing social media this way, it's probably not exciting to you either!

Let me give you an example. Let's say you sell weight loss products. If you post about your weight loss product every day, chances are your audience is going to get tired and eventually stop following your account. You'll "feel good" knowing you posted about your product that day—but truth be told, no one in your audience would "feel good" or engage with your content.

But what if instead you talked primarily about a healthy weight journey and what that looked like. And you gave many tips to engage new followers to learn from you?

That's why it's important that you know your WHO—who your ideal customer is. How can you serve them with content that attracts them rather than repels them? This is how you build your audience and attract the perfect potential customers. This way, when you sprinkle in your own product, you have more people who want to try, buy, or even learn more.

> **IT'S IMPORTANT THAT YOU KNOW YOUR WHO—WHO YOUR IDEAL CUSTOMER IS.**

If you get to know your "avatar" (your potential customer), you can actually be the place that people check on purpose for inspiration, motivation, and education! You want to think about what type of content they would enjoy. A lot of this can be found by checking your "insights" or by

SOCIAL MEDIA THAT SELLS:
MY SOCIAL MEDIA SELLING SYSTEM

creating an "avatar"—writing down who your ideal client is and thinking about content they would enjoy.

Let's use the example of weight loss and wellness. Most people could use your product. So, how do you introduce it without losing their interest up front?

Three words: *GIVE GREAT VALUE!*

Want to know how you outsmart the algorithm? Be the place people check *on purpose*! In other words, create content so good that people check your social media accounts every single day to see what you share—and then they share your content with their friends. This increases your exposure and that's what we teach our Network Marketing Inner Circle coaching clients.

> **CREATE CONTENT SO GOOD THAT PEOPLE CHECK YOUR SOCIAL MEDIA ACCOUNTS EVERY SINGLE DAY TO SEE WHAT YOU SHARE—AND THEN THEY SHARE YOUR CONTENT WITH THEIR FRIENDS.**

THE MULTIPLY METHOD

In order to be successful at "selling" on social media, you must create content that:
- Performs well with your audience
- Performs well with the algorithm

Creating Posts That Perform with Your Audience

When my Network Marketing Inner Circle clients say, "Sarah, I'm using the strategy you're teaching to get engagement, but I'd like to grow even faster," I usually respond: "Let's look at what you're posting. Are you giving your audience value? Are you making their lives easier or better? Is your content 'sharable'—meaning, is it interesting enough that they share it with their friend? If it's not, we need to go back to the drawing board."

Using the weight loss and wellness example, what are some things you could "talk" to your audience about that might interest them and attract new people? Here are some ideas:

- Healthy lunches
- High-protein snacks
- Increasing your water intake
- Fast, fun workouts
- Ways to get more steps in
- Favorite recipes
- Funny memes
- Inspiration (quotes)
- Motivation (stories)
- Education (tips)

SOCIAL MEDIA THAT SELLS: MY SOCIAL MEDIA SELLING SYSTEM

You see, when you're the place people check on purpose, not only can you outsmart the algorithm but you create the type of content your ideal customer will consume *and* share with others.

Workshop This

Who is my ideal client, and what type of content might they enjoy? What could some of my social media "pillars" (post topics) be:

-
-
-
-
-

Be a Giver of Great Value!

Here's a story of how I turned a simple Facebook page into a community with a social media following of over five hundred thousand people.

When I started my business, my company had a funny rule: We couldn't say our company name on social media. This actually ended up working to my benefit. I knew I wanted to use social media as a tool to not only share my business but also to serve people by sharing *how* I was growing my business. (I guess that's the former teacher in me!) I would go online every week and share my "prospecting pop-ups"—training tips in under ten minutes! I would share sales strategies, techniques, and ideas for growing a successful sales organization.

I gave such great value that not only did my team tune in, but people from other companies started sharing my content with others. Eventually, that page grew to over three hundred thousand people, and my collective social media following grew to over half a million! I was eventually able to monetize by releasing a book, offering coaching to people in the industry, and running a mastermind for top industry leaders. I do keynote speaking and consulting for companies too.

That's what people are doing today with live videos and podcasts—offering free value weekly to grow their audience. This is how you grow an audience, and it leads to sales.

Now, this may not be your audience (network marketers), but let's say you want to sell your product to potential customers. So what free tips can you give on social media to help them in the area where they're struggling? And how can your product be a solution for those problems on social? The answer is this: Pause before you post every day and ask yourself: *How can I make their lives easier or better today?* Think, *What can I give?* instead of *What can I get?*

I love this quote by Winston Churchill: "We make a living by what we get, but we make a life by what we give." This is certainly true with social media. It really is an upside-down approach—you have to give in order to get. And every post comes with a price: gained followers

SOCIAL MEDIA THAT SELLS:
MY SOCIAL MEDIA SELLING SYSTEM

(potential customers) or lost followers. So, be sure to "pause before you post" and "post on purpose." That's half the equation for success on social.

> BE SURE TO "PAUSE BEFORE YOU POST" AND "POST ON PURPOSE." THAT'S HALF THE EQUATION FOR SUCCESS ON SOCIAL.

Creating Posts That Perform in the Algorithm
In addition to creating posts that perform well with your audience, you must also create posts that perform well in the algorithm. I like to call this "social media's grading system," which determines who sees what you post.

As I mentioned earlier, the algorithm is changing all the time, so we will not go into specifics here. I cannot stress enough that if you want up-to-date coaching in a supportive community, you need to join us in the Network Marketing Inner Circle, where you'll get the best in social media strategy and network marketing systems and sales training.

THE MULTIPLY METHOD

However, a few things that will never change: Social media is a social platform. It's kind of like a jealous ex—it doesn't want you leaving or sending people other places. So, you must know how to play the game. Your ultimate goal is to get people to engage with your content (likes and loves, comments and conversation, saves and shares)—and the platform's goal is to get people to spend more time on the platform. It rewards you for that!

How do we do this? Let's talk strategy! In order to be successful selling on social, you must master the following four things:

1. Storytelling
2. Show + Tell
3. Sharing
4. Systems

Success in social media marketing is all about storytelling, not selling! The second you start posting links or sales language, not only does it turn off your audience—it also causes your post to perform poorly in social media's algorithm. Because it's all selling, social media suppresses that type of content.

So, how do we tell a story? Remember, we first want to focus on "value-add" posts. Posts that build our audience do so by adding value—which will cast a wider net. This way, when we post about our business or products, we reach more people who may be interested in trying,

SOCIAL MEDIA THAT SELLS:
MY SOCIAL MEDIA SELLING SYSTEM

buying, or learning more. Value-added posts should make up 9/10 of your posts.

If you're sprinkling in your business the other 1/10 of the time, how do you do this effectively? Again, you do it by storytelling—not selling! You can tell a story about your product by using:

- Before-and-after images: These are a great way to provide social proof!
- Progress photos
- Places your products have been featured in the media
- Awards won
- Testimonials
- Other people's stories about the business

As you know, you are "selling" two things: a product and an opportunity. How do you tell a story about the business opportunity? You do it by sharing

- Success stories ("In part-time hours, this business is allowing me to…")
- New distributor welcome posts (sharing WHY they joined, so others can relate)
- Recognition and rewards—and not just when they've been earned, but also when they're available to earn. (Some people will work harder for praise than raises.)
- Events and experiences—many join for community!

THE MULTIPLY METHOD

The idea is to create excitement by sharing experiences—not by presenting a constant sales pitch. Here are some great examples for your 1/10 business posts:

Power Post Examples
- **Before-and-After Pictures:** Showcase people who are using your products—or even post progress photos as they go. Talk to your audience about how to get these benefits.

- **Press:** When you're featured in the press or receive awards, shout it out! Share the publication or some quotes. Remember, people don't always want all the details; they simply want to know "Does it work?"

- **Testimonials:** To get a testimonial, it's as simple as messaging a customer and asking for their feedback. Just ask: "How are you loving your product?" When you get good feedback, ask for permission to shout it out and share with your audience. And then ask: "Who wants to get results like these?"

- **Success Stories and Welcoming New Partners:** Share their WHY and what the business is doing for them—or allowing them to do for others. This can attract people like them for whom the opportunity may benefit. I like to use this formula when telling someone else's story: "In part-time hours, the business allows her to…" Focus on meaning versus money. This builds belief!

SOCIAL MEDIA THAT SELLS: MY SOCIAL MEDIA SELLING SYSTEM

- **Recognition and Rewards:** Share not only when you earn them but also when they become available to earn. Too often distributors miss an opportunity when they think, *Well, I didn't earn it, so I shouldn't post about it!* Friend, the moment your company offers a perk, share it. You never know who will be interested. My friend joined because her upline posted about a free trip that could be earned—it caught her attention because she loves to travel!

- **Events and Experiences:** Some people get into the business for the community. Never underestimate the power of showcasing team events or company trips. Show how much fun you're having!

Speaking of showcasing the business on social, that brings me to my next rule for success in selling on social: *Show, don't tell!*

Let's dive into the three parts of my social media selling system:

- Create curiosity with engaging content.
- Engage people in the comments section.
- When they do, get in their inbox with our simple selling system.

THE MULTIPLY METHOD

Curiosity Marketing Converts to Customers! (My Content-to-Cash Formula)

Curiosity marketing is one of the most powerful tools you can use to generate interest and attract leads on social media. The idea is simple: Instead of directly promoting your product or opportunity, focus on creating intrigue and prompting questions from your audience. Rather than giving away all the details, leave just enough information to spark curiosity, which leads to more engagement and, ultimately, more people reaching out to you.

> **RATHER THAN GIVING AWAY ALL THE DETAILS, LEAVE JUST ENOUGH INFORMATION TO SPARK CURIOSITY, WHICH LEADS TO MORE ENGAGEMENT AND, ULTIMATELY, MORE PEOPLE REACHING OUT TO YOU.**

SOCIAL MEDIA THAT SELLS: MY SOCIAL MEDIA SELLING SYSTEM

When I share my product or opportunity on social media, I intentionally avoid using the company or product name. Instead, I share *stories* and *experiences* that highlight the transformation or benefits without revealing the exact details. For example, I might post a picture of a product in use, but not mention what it is. I might say something like, "This has been a total game-changer for my mornings! I can't believe how much energy I have now. Comment ENERGY below for more info!" My goal is to make people curious enough to ask, "What is it?" or "How do I get that?" This approach encourages them to come to *me* for the answers instead of me pushing the product or company on them.

Write this down: *Sell the benefits, don't tell us what it is!*

Here's another example: Let's say I'm sharing about a new collagen product. First, I share the benefits of collagen in general. Then, I highlight the benefits of our collagen product. Finally, I prompt them to comment or message the word "Collagen" to me for more information or a special offer.

This type of curiosity-based posting works wonders because it invites *dialogue*. Instead of just throwing information out there, you're creating a sense of mystery that people want to explore. When you post links, you don't know who clicked them to follow up. But when you invite them to comment or message you, not only does it boost engagement, it opens up the conversation so you can effectively follow up. You don't have to directly sell anything; you're simply opening the door for conversation. People can comment, DM you, or message you privately to learn more.

That's how I get leads coming to me. People feel like they're discovering something for themselves, which builds trust and a sense of ownership in the process. And when they reach out, they're already warm leads—interested and ready to know more.

Additionally, when you don't reveal the full details up front, you're also setting the stage for a personal, one-on-one conversation. This allows you to tailor your response to their specific needs, whether it's a product recommendation or an opportunity to join your team. It's much more effective than blasting out generic marketing messages, and it leads to stronger connections with potential customers or team members.

Leverage curiosity marketing to "brand the build"— and build value around the community you are creating (the opportunity) and the products you are using.

By using curiosity marketing, I've created a flow where my audience comes to me—not the other way around. They don't feel sold to! It's a game changer for building relationships and growing my business, all while keeping the process fun and authentic. The key is to create content that invites curiosity, and then be ready to engage and build trust with those who reach out.

SOCIAL MEDIA THAT SELLS:
MY SOCIAL MEDIA SELLING SYSTEM

Once you get people curious, you must get them commenting. Conversation is the currency of social media.

CONVERSATION IS THE CURRENCY OF SOCIAL MEDIA.

How to Boost Engagement on Social Media: Getting People into the Comments

One of the best ways to increase engagement on social media is by actively encouraging people to leave comments. Not only does this increase visibility for your posts, but it also allows you to connect with your audience in a more meaningful way. The key is to make your posts interactive and create opportunities for your followers to respond.

One simple but powerful tactic is ending your posts with a question. Questions invite conversation and prompt people to share their thoughts. For example, if you're posting about a healthy lifestyle product, you could say: "What's your go-to morning routine? Drop it in the comments!" This encourages followers to share their own experiences, and by engaging with their comments, you keep the conversation going.

Another effective technique is using a *one-word call to action*. For example, at the end of a post about the business, you could say, "Want to know more? Comment INSIDER below for exclusive info!" This makes it easy for people to engage without feeling overwhelmed. A simple comment like "INSIDER" can lead to a meaningful conversation when you follow up, and it's an easy way for your audience to take action without a huge commitment. It's also clear and direct, so followers know exactly what to do if they want more information.

Why Comment Engagement Boosts Your Social Media Success

When your followers engage in the comments, it doesn't just boost your visibility—it also boosts your algorithm ranking. Social media platforms like Instagram and Facebook prioritize posts with higher engagement. The more comments your post gets, the more likely it is to be seen by a larger audience. This creates a snowball effect where the more you engage, the more your content will be pushed to the forefront, attracting even more eyes to your profile.

Additionally, by getting people into the comments, you create a direct line of communication with potential customers or team members. Commenters are already showing interest, and this provides an opportunity for you to follow up with them in a personal and authentic

SOCIAL MEDIA THAT SELLS: MY SOCIAL MEDIA SELLING SYSTEM

way. For instance, if someone comments INSIDER on your post, you can reach out directly, thank them for commenting, and offer more details about the product or opportunity. This method feels more personalized and less "sales-y" than a generic message to your entire audience as you thank them for their interest.

When they do express interest in your product, what do you do next?

Convert Curiosity into Customers

When someone inquires about the product, respond with our simple social media selling system:

- **Recommendation:** "Thanks for your interest. If you could change one thing about your _____, what would it be?"

- **Validation:** "Here's what I recommend. Check out the results of our customers!" (Send before-and-after images or testimonials.) "You're going to love it!"

- **Enrollment:** "We have a special today that you're going to love." (Let them know about the special.) "With our guarantee of _____, you have nothing to lose. Would you like to give it a try?"

It really is that simple!

Here's a summary of how to sell on social: A post a day keeps leads coming your way—not all posts should be about your business! Every day, focus on giving great value. Think about your target audience or avatar (the person who needs your product). What problems do they face? Outside of your product, how can you solve them by sharing value on social media today? Remember, your product is only one solution to their problems. Ask yourself: *How can I make their lives easier or better today?* Be a source of inspiration, education, and motivation. Serve them on social media. You never have to worry about the algorithm if you are the place that people check on purpose! Every post comes with a price—you are either gaining or losing potential followers that day. And remember, followers are all potential customers!

> **BE A SOURCE OF INSPIRATION, EDUCATION, AND MOTIVATION.**

SOCIAL MEDIA THAT SELLS: MY SOCIAL MEDIA SELLING SYSTEM

Application

Who is your "who"? Think about your products. Who is the ideal customer?

_____

_____

What problems do they have?

_____

_____

_____

What type of content would they be interested in? What potential problems could you solve for them on social, other than selling them on your product?

_____

_____

_____

_____

THE MULTIPLY METHOD

> P.S. Social media is a great way to generate new leads for your network marketing business! To stay up-to-date with the latest in social media strategy and to learn how to professionally prospect on every single social media platform, join us for coaching at thenetworkmarketinginnercircle.com
>
> All companies welcome! No matter your level on social media, it will help you to level up!

Speaking of leveling up, I'm excited about what I'm going to share next: my system for duplicating leaders in our business. Spoiler alert: I believe this was one of the main reasons we created the fastest-growing sales team in the industry. It's all about leadership!

CHAPTER 8

LEADERSHIP SYSTEMS AND DUPLICATION: LET'S MULTIPLY!

ARE YOU READY to level up? If you are a leader or an aspiring leader who wants to build a successful, sustainable organization in your company, this chapter is for you!

In the business of duplication, you are only as successful as your team. It's not just what you do—but what you duplicate that leads to a solid, successful, sustainable sales team! The duplication systems I am about to teach you were responsible for creating one of the largest, most successful sales teams in the history of our industry, worldwide. When you unlock this, it will be a game changer for you.

There are three duplication systems you must master in order for your sales team to become successful:

1. All-Team Training
2. Aspiring Leader Training
3. All-Star (Leadership) Training

THE MULTIPLY METHOD

If you haven't yet built a team, put this in your filing cabinet for later and focus on the previous chapters to lay your foundation. But if you're a leader who's interested in bringing people up the ranks, this is for you.

(And by the way, if you are a leader in network marketing, be sure to apply for our Made to Multiply Mastermind, where we help six-figure leaders scale to six-figure months by creating custom duplication systems for their businesses and help them monetize and generate leads by building their personal brand.)

All-Team Training Systems

"Work with the willing, love the rest." While this quote sounds catchy, I don't exactly agree with it. I like to say, "Work with the working, and develop systems for the rest." That way, when people's timing changes, they can plug in and succeed.

The reality is, our business shouldn't be sponsor dependent; it should be systems dependent. So setting up simple systems for your team from the start ensures that everyone wins—no matter who sponsors who!

Our All-Team Training System consists of weekly calls:

1. An opportunity/orientation open house call (so they can simply "invite")

LEADERSHIP SYSTEMS AND DUPLICATION: LET'S MULTIPLY!

2. A weekly team training or touchbase call (so they can "learn as they earn")

Every week, for as long as I can remember, we asked our team to block out one hour for weekly "power hours," where all they had to do was *listen and learn* and *excite and invite*!

Opportunity/Orientation Open House

Every week, we kick off the evening with a fifteen-to-thirty-minute opportunity/orientation open house, which we later called "opportunity pop-ups" ("opp pops" for short). Today, we call them open houses. During this presentation the leader shares:

- **Their story:** their WHY and what the business is doing for them or allowing them to do for others

- **The company story:** more about the opportunity to join us in business

- **The product story:** more about our award-winning products

Every open house ends with a call to action for the two ways to join us:
1. As a customer to get the following benefits: _____.

2. As a business partner to get the following benefits: _____.

THE MULTIPLY METHOD

We then invite them to get back with the person who invited them to answer any questions and tell them how they wish to join. This plants the seed for our consultants on how to "close."

When we taught our teams the simple skill of inviting, we grew at a record-breaking pace. All they had to do was invite others to the weekly presentations. And the best part is, they never had to master presenting, as they could plug guests into these brief opportunity calls. By listening in every week, they also participated in a kind of orientation, helping them successfully learn to present the opportunity. Hearing the great stories also reinforced their belief.

After the call we would break, allowing them to reach back out to the guest they'd invited, answer any questions, and get them started. We coached them to say:

1. Thank you!
2. What questions do you have?
3. How would you like to get started—customer or partner?

If they joined the business, they were able to join us for the training call that would follow.

Weekly Training

We held our weekly training for about thirty minutes each week, hosted by top leaders in the company. We always focused on simple skill sets that would easily duplicate:

LEADERSHIP SYSTEMS AND DUPLICATION: LET'S MULTIPLY!

- Defining Your WHY + Goal Setting
- Crafting + Sharing Your Short Story
- Creating Your List + Inviting Language
- Presenting + Events
- Closing + Common Objections
- Fast Start: Start New Partners Strong
- Product Training + Customer Enrollments

Pro tip: If you lead a large organization, you may have many leaders hosting trainings calls or building out a training platform. In this case, you may have weekly "Team Touchbases" where you share:

- WIN: What's Important Now and what to focus on in the coming week or month
- WINS: recognition
- Who's WINNING: invite a guest trainer to share "what's working now!"

By hearing a different speaker each week, they would learn:

1. WIN: What's Important Now—company announcements and how to leverage what was happening in the company at the time
2. The presenter's short story, which built belief
3. Simple, duplicable training

Our weekly power hours were a staple of our team system. They created a simple, duplicable system for our entire team. It wasn't a heavy lift, as all leaders agreed to host and promote. In addition to All-Team calls, we had programs for aspiring leaders and for my All-Stars (key top leaders in the organization who led large parts of my organization).

Aspiring Leader Calls

You may start these when you see duplication happening on your team—until then, stick with the All-Team Training System. When you see promotions happening, you can implement this next system as leaders start moving up the ranks.

In addition to All-Team Training calls, I've always loved running programs for aspiring leaders.

One of the things I became known for in the industry and in my company was something called the "Future Fives" program. We got the name because Level 5 was an entry-level leadership title that people could run for, which helped them maximize our pay plan. Future Fives provided accountability and action. We met weekly for as little as six weeks and as long as twelve weeks at a time. The goal was to get to a leadership title called "Level 5."

Not only did Future Fives duplicate leaders, but it also drove activity in the early stages of business because people were so excited to qualify for the program. To qualify, you had to hit a certain title by a certain date, complete a

LEADERSHIP SYSTEMS AND DUPLICATION: LET'S MULTIPLY!

predetermined amount of activity (sales and team-building goals), and apply. In the application, you would commit to a certain amount of activity in the program and weekly calls, and the main goal was to help you reach the top of the plan.

Here's a copy of our aspiring leader contract to give you an idea of the commitment involved:

I AGREE TO:

Congratulations! You have been selected to participate in our Aspiring Leader program. This program is designed to help you build your business and strengthen your leadership through systems, strategy, activity, and accountability.

By participating, you will:

- Accelerate the pace of your business with accountability.
- Learn new insights and strategies that will help you fast-track your results.
- Strengthen your leadership skills.

Participation is a must! You will be expected to report your stats weekly: the new customers you've helped, the new business partners you've added to your team, and your title promotions. All three will be assigned points and recognition, and prizes will be awarded at the end of the session. Your ultimate goal is to rise up the ranks of leadership!

To maximize what this program has to offer, you must be willing to commit to the following:

__ I will commit to following proven systems shared to sell, sponsor, and support my team.

__ I will work to sponsor ___ new business partners each month.

__ I will work to sponsor ___ new customers each month.

__ I commit to plugging into the trainings included in the program.

I am committed and accountable!

Name _____

Signature _____

THE MULTIPLY METHOD

Once accepted into the program, you would receive an accountability partner and commit to weekly calls during the series. We assign accountability partners because when you are accountable to someone, you are far more likely to go the distance and take the program seriously.

> **WHEN YOU ARE ACCOUNTABLE TO SOMEONE, YOU ARE FAR MORE LIKELY TO GO THE DISTANCE AND TAKE THE PROGRAM SERIOUSLY.**

Every week, the call would go something like this:

1. Accountability Partners (APs) share stats.
2. Top APs in points share best practices (peer learning).
3. Host shares a training tip and closes with a call to action/challenge.

LEADERSHIP SYSTEMS AND DUPLICATION: LET'S MULTIPLY!

We always opened the call with our stats. One person per accountability group would share:

- The number of new customers
- The number of new business partners
- Any promotions in title

After we shared stats, the top APs in points that week would share best practices—what was working for them! This peer learning was so powerful, as you could get great tips from others who were growing their business in real time. We would then conclude with some sort of training or tip for the week, along with a weekly challenge. The tip would be something to help them build their business and reach their goal.

At the end of the program, we would track points, and the top teams would get a prize. But the ultimate prize was promoting in the pay plan! Many of our top leaders came out of that program. And the program was so successful that most of the participants promoted to Level 5. When I saw many of the leaders on my teams at conventions or events, they told me: "I was a part of your Future Fives program—that changed everything for me!"

When our mastermind members deploy this program, they have massive success in their companies too! The program combines accountability with activity, which helps you develop top leaders. Remember, this shouldn't be overwhelming, as you're likely touching base with them already—but this system helps you be more intentional and strategic with your time.

Working with Your All-Stars

"You're only as successful as your leaders!" This was ingrained in me by every mentor I've had in the business—and it echoes the importance of duplicating leaders. For this reason, I have always had leadership communication channels and one-on-one touchpoints with the most influential leaders in my organization. I love to do this on a monthly basis with my monthly "Power Shot" strategy sessions.

> # YOU'RE ONLY AS SUCCESSFUL AS YOUR LEADERS!

Monthly Power Shots
One of the most valuable things you can do for your organization is stay in touch with the leaders on your sales team. That is why we meet on a monthly basis for Power Shot strategy sessions. This is when I meet with key leaders (personally sponsored or responsible for

LEADERSHIP SYSTEMS AND DUPLICATION: LET'S MULTIPLY!

large pockets of people within our sales organization) to reflect on the previous month, set goals for the current month, and discuss any strategies they need to succeed. In these hour-long meetings, we look at:

- The previous month's sales (personal and team)
- The previous month's sponsoring (personal and team)
- Any personal title or program goals

Then we look at the month ahead and set goals:

- Personal + Team Sales Goals
- Personal + Team Sponsoring Goals
- Any Personal Program or Promotion Goals

At the end of the meeting, we strategize and plan. I like to ask two questions at this point:

- Are there any leaks in your pipeline as it relates to personal belief, skill set, or desire?
- What can I help you work through this month?

And then we work through these things. I truly believe coaching can be conversational and doesn't require preplanning on your part. Instead, your partner shows up prepared for the call. It also keeps them measuring KPIs (key performance indicators) so they can control what's happening in their business.

THE MULTIPLY METHOD

To help you with these monthly Power Shot strategy sessions with your key leaders, I've included our goal-setting sheet that I have my power partners fill out prior to the session.

Your name_____ Date_____

GOAL SETTING

Please fill out this form on the first of each month and share it with your accountability partner and/or sponsor.

How Did You Close the Month? (Month in Review)

Your Personal Sales from Last Month: $_____

Your Team Sales from Last Month: $_____

Your Personal Sponsoring from Last Month:_____

Your Team Sponsoring from Last Month:_____

Program Goals/Achievements Made: _____

Are there any leaks in your pipeline?=> Desire___Belief___Skill___
If so, what solutions can we discuss to overcome them? Share below.

This Month's Goals (Setting Goals for the Current Month)
Commit Your Numbers

Your Personal Sales GOAL for This Month: $_____

Your Team Sales GOAL for This Month: $_____

Your Personal Sponsoring GOAL for This Month: _____

Your Team Sponsoring GOAL for This Month: _____

Program GOALS/Title GOALS for This Month: _____

What is your team currently working on? How can I help?

LEADERSHIP SYSTEMS AND DUPLICATION: LET'S MULTIPLY!

This meeting allows us to set goals for the upcoming month and measure the previous month against the goals set prior. These KPIs help you treat your business like a business and keep a good pulse on your organization at all times, setting growth goals rather than letting the business slip away. This also creates a cohesive relationship with your leaders by staying in contact and being strategic with them.

What I love about these leader calls is that they don't require preparation. Your leaders are coming with their own numbers, goals, and what they wish to work on, making it a positive, productive discussion.

I'm super proud of the relationship I've built with my key leaders—mainly because we've been so connected and strategic over the years! Give it a try—I think you'll be pleased at how simple, yet effective, this system is. And how easy it is to duplicate.

Duplication = Multiplication!
In our business, momentum is created by a lot of people, each doing a little bit more. Truth be told, you'd likely rather be paid a little bit on a lot of people's efforts than 100 percent of your own on your very best day. So be sure to put success systems in place that keep things simple but help them to duplicate.

> **MOMENTUM IS CREATED BY A LOT OF PEOPLE, EACH DOING A LITTLE BIT MORE.**

Start with team training and onboarding. Next, focus on opportunity/orientation calls. Then go from there. You'll know you're ready for the next steps to scale when your growth starts outpacing you.

Let's Multiply!

In the next chapter, we'll talk about how to create culture and communicate—because it truly is the glue that keeps your team together for the long term. It starts on day one—and with you. And it's something everyone will benefit from.

LEADERSHIP SYSTEMS AND DUPLICATION: LET'S MULTIPLY!

Application

Based on what you learned about leadership systems, what will you *start* doing, what will you *stop* doing, and what will you *continue* to do?

- Start _____

    _____

- Stop _____

    _____

- Continue _____

    _____

> If you are a leader who leads a large team, has hit top ranks, and could benefit from a top leader mastermind with peer collaboration, we can help you create a custom onboarding and duplication system for your team. Be sure to apply to our Made to Multiply Mastermind!

CHAPTER 9

CREATING TEAM CULTURE: THE GLUE THAT HOLDS THE TEAM TOGETHER

LET'S HAVE SOME real talk.

There is so much hype in our industry. That's why I always lead with truth. I believe *the truth is good enough.* If this is not the culture your company has, create it. Culture on your team starts with you. Culture is something *you* create.

> **CULTURE ON YOUR TEAM STARTS WITH YOU. CULTURE IS SOMETHING YOU CREATE.**

THE MULTIPLY METHOD

Culture is the glue that holds your team together—in both the good times and the tough times. In *every* business, there will be ups and downs—challenges and achievements. Creating a strong team culture will be what sustains you through all seasons of business.

Spoiler alert: No company stays in hyper-growth mode forever. There hasn't ever been one that has. I know—many of you think you will be the exception to the rule. But the reality is, this industry has been around for over one hundred years, and there are enough examples to show you that you won't be the exception. Just like the economy, there will be ups and downs.

This is why true leaders play the long game. I coach my students to pick one company, stick with that one company, build it to the very top, and play the long game. Much like the economy, business goes through different growth seasons.

I know we'd all like to believe that our company or business will forever be in momentum mode. But take it from someone who's been in the profession for two decades and coached leaders across different companies in our masterminds: No company, no leader, stays in momentum forever. It's not if, it's when. And I believe more people need to tell the truth about that. It's how your team will stick with you when there are changes and challenges. Because you are a leader who tells the truth.

CREATING TEAM CULTURE: THE GLUE THAT HOLDS THE TEAM TOGETHER

I always say: "You don't need a new opportunity—you need a new commitment to the opportunity you've been given."

> **YOU DON'T NEED A NEW OPPORTUNITY—YOU NEED A NEW COMMITMENT TO THE OPPORTUNITY YOU'VE BEEN GIVEN.**

One of my mentors is Donna Johnson. Donna is celebrating four decades with her company. I've watched the industry evolve over time, and Donna has remained steady. She has experienced success compounded over time.

Donna always reminds me: "Sarah, I know people who would be millionaires today if they simply hadn't quit." Leaders play the long game. Leaders lead with legacy in mind. True leaders learn the industry, understand this, and coach their teams confidently through trying times—because in every company, those times will come.

THE MULTIPLY METHOD

And for the love—when you see the smoke and mirrors and hype on social media, know it's just that: *marketing*. Don't be distracted by shiny objects. Stay focused. A good leader will always support you in your business and affirm and respect your decision to stay with your company. Pick a company and stick with it. Give it the time that it takes. Build it straight to the top. That's how you create legacy.

Last (and I added this after my company of twenty years closed its doors to distributors), lean into leadership in good times and in hard times. Because I was actively leading in every season (on the mountain and in the valley), that is what allowed me to build my second business faster than the first one. Leaders who get into "legacy leader mode" and stop leading don't get that second strong chance.

OK, I'm off my soapbox. But someone had to tell the truth! I hate the hype. And I feel so called to redeem this industry and preserve the legacy of our profession.

So, how do you keep your team intact during tough times and together during celebratory times?

Team culture is created by two things:

- Communication
- Community

Both communication and community make a team *unstoppable*.

CREATING TEAM CULTURE: THE GLUE THAT HOLDS THE TEAM TOGETHER

BOTH COMMUNICATION AND COMMUNITY MAKE A TEAM UNSTOPPABLE.

Communication

From the beginning of building my business, we created such an unstoppable team culture that people outside of our team wanted to be a part of it—this is why I share what I know with the industry. I've always operated out of an abundance mindset: *A healthy company and profession is healthy for us all!* I share a wealth of free resources at SarahRobbins.com. As a side note, this has served me well: I'm now a trusted coach, consultant, and keynote speaker for distributors and companies across the profession and beyond.

As for our company systems, I've kept our channels of communication open to all consultants on our team—from our trainings and newsletters to team pages/groups and events. I operate from a place of total abundance. This approach has blessed not only our company but also my team and me. I could write a whole book on this. Give out of abundance, and you will grow.

THE MULTIPLY METHOD

Now, let's explore the elements that make these communication channels successful:

- **Weekly Calls + Events:** As mentioned in the previous chapter, your core team system will thrive when you incorporate regular touchpoints for training and opportunity-type events. These also serve as orientations to the company story and showcase top leaders' stories to build belief. This simple system helped us grow a team that broke records in our industry. Remember, we signed up three hundred people in one month—and then went on to build a team of over three hundred thousand and do nearly $3 billon in sales one year—and all people had to do was *invite*.

- **Newsletters:** These are a great way to provide monthly recognition and weekly communication, sharing team calls and "WIN" (What's Important Now). You can highlight your superstar sellers and rockstar recruiters, welcome your newbies, and showcase promotions and recognition. Newsletters are also a great place to share any team trainings, monthly incentives, and contests. If most people who join your business are part-timers, this keeps them plugged in.

- **Team Pages/Groups/Chats:** Initially, I recommend starting with a team communication thread, which can later grow into larger team groups. These are places to post trainings, recognize your team, welcome new people, and share announcements. Think of it as gathering your team "around the water cooler"—plus, it's a great way for your team to connect and develop a sense of community. When the chat gets too busy, that's a sign it's time to move on to a team page.

Community + Experiences

Company Events

Company events are a great way to experience company culture and get a bigger picture of what's possible. I always attend company events and promote them—whether they're for a new person (I, too, can always learn something new) or for the aspiring leader. These events are incredibly aspirational. Many of our team leaders say their belief was built during an event. Plus, they're a great way to meet people and establish deeper relationships. Company events can include Super Saturday trainings, conventions, and leadership summits. And don't just announce them—be sure to promote them!

Retreats

I love hosting retreats for my team. They don't have to cost a lot, especially if people pay their own way, but they are always a good investment of time. Time is the currency of relationships, and we are in the relationship business. Your team bonds and builds during the time you spend with them.

For example, my sister hosted a one-day event focused on business and brand building. It included brunch and a brainstorming session where everyone shared a best practice and one thing about which they wanted to brainstorm. Then they offered professional headshots, followed by a fun night of bonding around a bonfire. Everyone paid their way, and she hosted a brunch buffet with yogurt, boiled eggs, fruit, and coffee.

I've hosted large-scale retreats with a Friday night icebreaker (we've done chef dinners with icebreaker questions and scavenger hunts at a local mall, which were a blast). Saturday is usually our brunch and brainstorm (mastermind) day, where everyone shares a best practice (what's working) and one thing about which they want to brainstorm. We end the day with a celebration—this could be as fancy or as fun as you'd like. One of my favorites was when we had a barbecue in my backyard with a DJ, and we ended with a dance party. You could also host a dinner that ends with a pajama party! On Sunday, we close with an optional sunrise service. You can always incorporate fun recognition too.

Recognition
I always say: "People will work harder for praise than for raises." Recognition doesn't have to cost anything, but the rewards are priceless. I love recognizing:

CREATING TEAM CULTURE: THE GLUE THAT HOLDS THE TEAM TOGETHER

- Superstar sellers
- Rock-star recruiters
- Promotions and program achievers
- Newbie "knockouts"—new people who did something notable
- Team spirit award winners—people who add value to the team

> **PEOPLE WILL WORK HARDER FOR PRAISE THAN FOR RAISES.**

Recognition can happen in:
- Newsletters
- Team groups
- Team meetings
- Social media (both your team's and your own)

Recognition goes a long way! This mantra applies not just to your customers, but to your team too. *Treat them like royalty, and they will give you loyalty.*

THE MULTIPLY METHOD

Incentives

Let me assure you: You do not need to reinvent the wheel! I love anchoring into company incentive programs and driving achievement and recognition around them whenever possible. However, I like sprinkling in my own incentives too. Here are some ideas for incentive programs:

- **Month-End Momentum:** Have a sales goal you're going for? Do a countdown that unlocks a prize! For instance, X regimens sold gets us to our goal, so we are going to count back by fifty and when we get to zero, it unlocks a prize! This could be a random drawing or raffle or something like, when we get there, we all earn a special virtual celebration or call. I often help a leader host one of these events when they are earning their "team trophy" (such as their company vehicle), to get the team in on the fun—and of course, we do a fun "Dreaming + Driving" day for all!

- **Title Goals:** Help enough people get what they want, and this helps you achieve what you want. In our business, your success can never be about *you*. That's why you have to set growth goals with your team and focus on the rewards that they achieve when they get there. If there is none built in internally, create something you can work on together. "When you achieve _____, you get _____!" Maybe it's a bonus or prize.

CREATING TEAM CULTURE: THE GLUE THAT HOLDS THE TEAM TOGETHER

- **Raffles/Contests:** Activity is the cure to what ails you in your business. Too often, top leaders make the mistake of only rewarding achievements—but what if you started rewarding activity? After all, activity leads to outcomes. That is why I love raffles where they get points toward a prize draw. For example, 1 new customer = 1 entry; 1 new team member = 2 entries; 1 promotion = 3 entries. Or base it on activity: host an event and post the event, get an entry. And so on!

- **Beat Your Best:** When you have a great month, focus the next month on beating the previous month's sales. When your team accomplishes this, they can shout it out—and they can earn special recognition. (All who "beat their best" achieve _____!)

- **Title Promotions:** As you grow, host celebrations or special dinners during your company events, or host your own events. Leadership retreats are awesome too. Set a qualification date that will drive natural momentum within your organization.

- **VIP Club:** This is a great way to drive overall team achievement. Take whatever your company sales are for the minimum promotions and when people hit it, put their "name in lights"—give them recognition and feature them on a monthly celebratory call with raffles and a special night of training. You could also host a virtual "red carpet" recognition event.

THE MULTIPLY METHOD

Now, I'm not suggesting that you do all of these things—I don't do all of them at any given time—but focus on one at a time and do them when needed. Be strategic about when you host your own incentives based on the team goals. It's so much fun to reward and recognize people on your team!

Now let's talk about more fun ways to reward and recognize. Remember, people will often work harder for praise than for raises—some run for bigger paychecks, but many run for fun team and company promotions. Here are some favorite ideas for incentives:

- Coffee Gift Cards: "You're a star, here are some bucks! Let's keep business brewing!"

- Lunch with a Leader: Time spent together talking vision and strategy is always a great investment.

- Customized Swag: Let them rep their team, your team, or the company.

- Complimentary Samples: The gift that keeps on giving, as it also grows the business!

- Shopping Sprees/Gift Cards: These can be small, but they're always meaningful and fun!

- Celebratory Dinners: These can be just for your team, or you can anchor them on to larger events.

- Social Media Recognition: People love to see their "name in lights"!

CREATING TEAM CULTURE: THE GLUE THAT HOLDS THE TEAM TOGETHER

- Celebratory Calls with Prize Raffles: Every month, add special recognition to your meetings.

- Team Parties: These are always a fun way to celebrate, especially with creative themes!

A team who plays together stays together. Not only is recognition an important part of your team culture, it's a wise investment of time and resources (plus, it's a write-off for your business).

Two More Aspects of Team Culture: Collaboration and Connection!

Along with the fundamentals, I want to talk about the key principles of building team culture and creating camaraderie that I've found incredibly valuable over the years: *collaboration and connection.*

Collaboration

We are better together—this should be the ongoing theme of every touchpoint with your team. *Everyone believes when everyone buys in!* Finding a role for your team members is key when creating an unstoppable culture plus commitment.

In the beginning, what that looked like for me was making sure everyone on our team who wished to play a part in team meetings was able to. This way, they not only

THE MULTIPLY METHOD

showed up, but also invited guests. Everyone who wanted a role had one, and these roles included:

- Greeters
- Product Setup Crew
- Enrollment Station Crew
- Registration Table Crew
- Presenters
- Trainers
- Storytellers (Product + Business)
- Closers

Now, as I lead a large, global organization, I do this on a leadership level. Not only do we brainstorm on process together, but we implement together by:

- Sharing our stories on weekly calls
- Taking turns hosting weekly trainings

In addition, we all agree to host and promote! This has created momentum on our teams. When people buy in to the vision, they believe!

WHEN PEOPLE BUY IN TO THE VISION, THEY BELIEVE!

CREATING TEAM CULTURE: THE GLUE THAT HOLDS THE TEAM TOGETHER

Connection

Connection is also a big part of creating culture. We love to create team culture by fostering community. This has looked like special team toasts or parties tacked on to corporate events, as well as inclusion activities: "Wear an orange ribbon on your name tag so we can high-five you and hug you!" We've also hosted fun activities like pajama parties.

Remember—people join our business for financial opportunity, but they often stay for the fun and the friendships. I've made lifelong friends in our business. When you create a "better together" business model, you create a team that will stand the test of time. It's one of the most important things you will ever do.

Take a few minutes and ask yourself these two questions: *What kind of leader do I want to be known for? What kind of team culture do I want to create?* Don't wait for someone else to do it. As my mentor would say: Be the leader you want to follow!

> # BE THE LEADER YOU WANT TO FOLLOW!

Customer service isn't just for your customers—it's also about the experience you create for your teams. Remember, the culture that you create starts with *you*!

THE MULTIPLY METHOD

Application

Based on what you learned in this chapter, what do you want to *start* doing, *stop* doing, and *continue* to do?

- Start

_____

_____

- Stop

_____

_____

- Continue

_____

_____

CONCLUSION

YOU WERE MADE TO MULTIPLY!

You made it! You've read through the systems, the strategies, and the steps to building a successful network marketing business. But now, the real question is: Will you put the systems, strategies, and steps into action?

I know what you're thinking: *This is going to be a lot of heavy lifting!* But let me clarify—this work won't necessarily be hard, but it will require consistent effort. Daily prospecting, presenting, closing, and getting people off to a great start—this is the heart of the Multiply Method. Simple systems always work—if you work them.

Will it be easy? No. You'll have to put in the work, but let me ask you some important questions: Will it be worth it? What is your WHY worth? If time and money were no object, how would you live? What would you give? How would you spend your money and time?

Imagine a life where you live more, give more, and love your life even more. This is what you're working toward. When I started my business, there were plenty of moments when I wanted to quit, but I stayed clear on my WHY—and it kept me going.

Early on, a mentor asked me, "Sarah, what's your WHY?" I replied, "I want to start a foundation for women and children." She then asked, "How much will that cost?" I hesitated before answering, "Millions!" Her next question changed everything: "So, how does that feel?"

I remember feeling overwhelmed. I didn't know where to begin. But my mentor gave me invaluable advice: Break your big WHY into smaller, more manageable goals. So I decided that instead of focusing on millions, I'd focus on helping one family at a time. Every month, I set aside a portion of my paycheck to do something meaningful— pay medical bills for a family, buy groceries for someone in need, send kids of a single mom to camp. And as my income grew, so did my impact.

We started by supporting families and, over time, we built homes overseas for children in need. We even gifted our first family home to a deserving family, free of charge. But here's the truth: *It wasn't always easy.*

I'll never forget one particularly difficult season when I found myself crying, sitting on my faux-leather couch, tears pooling on that pleather finish, thinking, *God, I don't want to do this. I didn't ask for this.* And then, in the quiet, I heard a voice say, "It's not about you. It's about the people who will be blessed through you."

CONCLUSION: YOU WERE MADE TO MULTIPLY!

I'm so grateful I didn't quit. We've changed countless lives along the way. And we've modeled generosity as our legacy to our children.

Your legacy is tied to your willingness to say yes every day—even on the hard days. Remember, your blessings and the blessings of others are connected to your obedience. So when you hit those tough moments—when the grind feels too much, when things seem to be moving slowly—don't quit. Give yourself one year to see what your business can do. Will it be easy? No. But will it be worth it? Well, the answer to that can be answered with this question: What is your WHY worth?

> **YOUR LEGACY IS TIED TO YOUR WILLINGNESS TO SAY YES EVERY DAY— EVEN ON THE HARD DAYS.**

There are seasons of difficulty in every journey. *Pick your hard.* Which is harder: building your business and designing a life that fits around the rest of your life, or staying in the 9-to-5 grind where you trade hours for dollars, work until dark, and barely have enough to get by, let alone live the life you truly want or leave a legacy?

THE MULTIPLY METHOD

Pick your hard. Nothing we do here is difficult—it just requires discipline. And that discipline pays off in the most incredible ways: time freedom, financial freedom, and the ability to design a life you love and leave a legacy.

When the doors of my business closed, I stood at a crossroads. It was a defining moment in my life. I could have walked away, chosen something completely different, or even retired. But in that moment, I knew this wasn't the end. It was the beginning.

I wasn't starting from scratch. I was starting with the lessons I'd learned, the systems that had once built a $1 billion sales team, and the unwavering belief that we could do this again. This wasn't about money. This was about legacy. About doing something that would change lives, that would create an impact that would outlast me. And most importantly, this was about my family and our legacy. The future I wanted for them was too important to walk away from.

So I chose to start again. To rebuild. To multiply what we had already accomplished, knowing we had something rare: a proven blueprint, the drive to push through the hardest moments, and the unshakeable will to succeed. Not to mention, the best business model on the planet. I took the chance to take our proven systems and partner with some of the best leaders in the industry and rewrite the story. We continue to multiply on a scale that will change lives and leave a legacy. And I can't wait to watch you do the same.

CONCLUSION: YOU WERE MADE TO MULTIPLY!

If you lock into one company, learn the systems, and implement them consistently, chapter by chapter, your success is inevitable. It is my honor to help you walk out your WHY!

What's Next?

What comes next after reading this book? What can you do to make the Multiply Method work for you? Here's what I recommend:

1. **Revisit your WHY.** Create a goal board with visuals so you're constantly reminded of your purpose. Write it down, share it, and live it. Then commit to the "WIT" mentality—*whatever it takes*. Never quit on a bad day. Remember, there are no emergencies in this business. You're building something for the long term, so what if it takes five, ten, or even fifteen years? Where else can you compress a thirty-to-fifty-year career into just a few short years? Your WHY is worth it!

2. **Set clear goals.** Then share them with someone who can hold you accountable. What help do you need? What daily activities do you need to commit to, and by when? A goal without a deadline is just a dream—so put it into action with a specific timeline.

THE MULTIPLY METHOD

3. **Daily activity is key.** Activity is the cure for what ails you. Start simple—make one social post today, share your business with one new person, and don't forget the follow-up. Consistency is everything!

4. **Read, review, and revisit the chapters in this book.** Revisit chapters 1 through 3 until this process becomes second nature to you. Once you've mastered those, dive into chapters 4 through 9. If you're a leader, form a book club with your team. The more people who understand the system, the faster your team will grow.

5. **Give it time.** You must become a student of this system. Give yourself grace to grow!

If you're looking for additional support and mentorship as you implement these steps, I invite you to consider joining one of our communities. Being part of a supportive network of like-minded individuals can dramatically accelerate your growth and success.

Hiring a coach saves you time and makes you money. It saves you time by shortening your learning curve and makes you money because you can finally implement the strategy you need to succeed. Think of it as a return on investment. And think of the power as we implement this system together!

We have a variety of groups where we dive deeper into the systems, provide ongoing training, share best practices, and hold each other accountable. These

CONCLUSION: YOU WERE MADE TO MULTIPLY!

communities are built to empower you with the resources you need to stay consistent and focused—whether you're just getting started or you're scaling your business to the next level. These communities are outlined in detail at the end of this book.

Joining a community isn't just about getting answers; it's about creating connections, finding inspiration, and learning how to level up alongside others who are on the same journey. Together, we can grow faster, achieve more, and push past the challenges that may otherwise hold us back.

If you feel ready to be part of something bigger—if you're ready to have accountability, ongoing learning, and a network that supports you every step of the way—then I'd love to invite you to plug into one of our communities. Scan this QR code or visit SarahRobbins.com to learn more about how you can get involved.

THE MULTIPLY METHOD

I'm excited to help you walk out your WHY!

You can do this! If a shy schoolteacher with no network can do it, so can you. Stay consistent. Follow the system. Your success will be directly related to your ability to find others who believe in the vision and share this simple system with them. The world is full of people just like you—people who are waiting for someone to show them a way forward. It's your job to find them. And if you keep sharing, I guarantee you *will* find them.

> THE WORLD IS
> FULL OF PEOPLE
> JUST LIKE YOU—
> PEOPLE WHO ARE
> WAITING FOR SOMEONE
> TO SHOW THEM
> A WAY FORWARD.
> IT'S YOUR JOB
> TO FIND THEM.

CONCLUSION: YOU WERE MADE TO MULTIPLY!

This profession is one of the greatest gifts we can offer to others. Network marketing truly is the great equalizer. It doesn't matter your background, your experience, or where you've come from. If you're coachable and committed, you can succeed.

Wishing you great success!
You were Made to Multiply!

XO,
Sarah

> For additional
> coaching information
> with Sarah and
> the Multiply Group,
> turn to page 227.

WAYS TO WORK WITH SARAH AND THE MULTIPLY GROUP

IF YOU'RE READY to take your network marketing business to the next level, there are multiple ways to work with me and the Multiply Group. Whether you're just getting started, you're a leader who's looking to multiply, or you need expert guidance for your company, we're here to support your journey.

1. **Download our FREE guide with prospecting tips and scripts.** If you want to power up your prospecting and rock your recruiting—or if you're just looking to sharpen your skills for selling and sponsoring, start with our FREE prospecting guide! This guide is packed with valuable tips and scripts that will help you generate more leads and start building relationships that turn into lasting customers and business partners. Download it now at ProspectingGuide.com.

THE MULTIPLY METHOD

2. **Build to your first six-figure year with our coaching community.** Are you ready to build your first six-figure year in network marketing? Join our coaching community, the Network Marketing Inner Circle, and get access to proven systems, strategies, and tools that will help you grow your business faster and smarter. With personalized coaching on sales, sponsoring, social media, and systems—and alongside a network of like-minded individuals—you'll have everything you need to turn your vision into reality. The Inner Circle is open to anybody, any company! Learn more at TheNetworkMarketingInnerCircle.com.

3. **Scale to six-figure months with our mastermind.** For those of you who are already seeing success and are ready to scale even further, our Made to Multiply Mastermind is the place for you. If you're a leader looking to scale your income from six figures per year to six figures per month, this high-level mastermind will help you create rapid growth strategies and systems to maximize your impact. Apply today at MadetoMultiply.com.

4. **Consulting and keynote speaking for companies.** Are you a business or company looking to scale to the next level? We specialize in helping organizations and companies create strategies for massive growth. Our team has consulted with businesses

WAYS TO WORK WITH SARAH AND THE MULTIPLY GROUP

ranging from startups to billion-dollar brands, and we can help you accelerate your success. If you're interested in working with us for consulting or keynote speaking opportunities, inquire today to learn how we can help you reach your full potential. Contact us at SarahRobbins.com.

No matter where you are on your journey, we have the tools, training, and support to help you achieve your biggest goals. Remember, success is a journey, not a destination. So, let's take the next step together.

> # REMEMBER, SUCCESS IS A JOURNEY, NOT A DESTINATION.

We look forward to working with you and seeing you MULTIPLY!